Let's Party
New Jersey's Top Places

For Catered Affairs

BAKIE & BAKIE

Let's Party
New Jersey's Top Places for Catered Affairs

©2007 by NJR Publications
118 Pine Bank Road
Flemington, New Jersey 08822
www.njrpublications.com

ISBN 978-0-9774068-1-4

Art Directors: G & G Graphics

On the cover: Party scenes photographed by Peter Wallburg Studios www.peterwallburgstudios.com

Printed on Acid Free Paper

Printed in the United States of America

1 2 3 4 5 6 7 8 9 0

Contents

Introduction

Life is full of momentous occasions to be celebrated. In this book we explore a host of premier locations available to mark those important events. From intimate to all out grand affairs, this book explores New Jersey's most fascinating venues to host a catered affair. Sail across the Hudson or gaze out at the Atlantic Ocean. Whether you are throwing a party for two or a thousand or more, discover the most elegant, most unique, and most dramatic places for a world-class celebration.

Everybody enjoys a party and whether you will be celebrating soon or in the future, we hope to give you a fascinating look at celebrating in style. From a party aboard ship to one surrounded by beautiful gardens, we present six chapters full of New Jersey's most fascinating locations to host a catered affair. In *Distinguished Elegance* it is opulence and palatial structures that create a sophisticated atmosphere for commemorating life's most important moments. Glistening chandeliers, lavish decorations, white glove service, and butler served hors d'oeuvres–it's all part of the experience.

With A View takes you through a host of dramatic facilities. The commonality is they all feature something for the eyes to behold. From panoramic waterscapes and cityscapes to the enchanting rolling fairways of a well groomed golf course, you will be captivated by the view.

Chapter three offers a tour of thrilling establishments. Big, bold, and exciting–places featured in this chapter will amaze you with sprawling ballrooms, marvelous fountains, and elaborate architecture. Each facility in this chapter promises a *Grand Experience*.

Pristine Surroundings will engulf you in the scenic beauty of picturesque gardens and lush greenery. Colorful, vibrant, and exuberating–there will be a festive mood in the air. Inside and out these fabulous locations will provide the atmosphere for enjoyment and celebration.

We all have birthdays, anniversaries, and many other milestones to mark in a special way. Explore *Intimate Celebrations* for spectacular options to do so. You will find everything from private rooms and communal tables to overnight stays and tableside service.

What's a party without *Culinary Pleasures*? Chapter six will introduce you to sinful gastronomic delights. Remarkable cuisine, meticulous service, and much more is offered from the extraordinary locations in chapter six.

From creating unusual venues to using the great outdoors, caterers are visionaries in their own right. With beautiful architectural structures, manicured gardens, elaborately presented cuisine, theatrical entertainment, and impeccable gracious service, caterers produce a high energy environment apropos of an all out celebration. This unique publication highlights the *crème de le crème* in catering. These facilities are top in their field and know how to orchestrate a magnificent affair. Take a tantalizing look at their culinary skills and pristine surroundings. Take an engaging tour of their facilities. See how these industry leaders have a fascinating ability to glorify important celebrations, rev up a party, and fill an evening with added excitement.

Use this book to show off your wedding site or decorate a coffee table. We hope you use it over and over again. Show off to your friends and family where you had your last special occasion. We were inspired to publish this book by our own search for a great place to throw a party. A fun and memorable look at New Jersey's top places for a catered affair was our mission.

The best party is just pages away. Enjoy.

Wine courtesy of Fiorino located in Summit. Photography by David Verdini Studios.

*A toast
to your next celebration,
may it bring
many lasting memories
to be cherished
for a lifetime.*

Chapter 1

Set in a quiet country setting, The Rockleigh is an ideal spot for social and corporate functions. The bea

Distingui

s guests into an atmosphere of old world charm and elegance.

Elegance

The Bristol Lobby (above) and an outdoor ceremony (left).

The Rockleigh

$\mathcal{T}$he Rockleigh is nestled in the heart of historic Rockleigh. It is a shining example of the town's old-world charm and timeless appeal. The Puccio Family became the proud owners in the fall of 1995. Jerry Puccio, Sr. recalls, "We were drawn to the town's

Willie Randolph and his daughter, Taniesha, celebrate.

rustic pleasures and historical significance. Though the club had long been established as a Bergen County country club, we had a vision to make this club the premier setting for weddings, bar/bat mitzvahs and corporate events.

"We understand the importance of your special event and always endeavor to make it uniquely yours. For your individual and specific needs, our banquet managers will custom design a menu that will be truly satisfying. The finest cuisine is prepared by our talented chefs and impeccably served by our experienced wait staff.

"At The Rockleigh, we take pride in our sense of family. Everyone works together, like a family,

The Grand Pavilion.

to ensure that your special day is a joyous and memorable one. Our professional staff, each with their own area of expertise, will bestow the care and concern you deserve. We look forward to serving you and your guests"

Your wedding day is one to cherish and remember. The Rockleigh has everything you need for an unforgettable affair. As you enter their wrought iron and stone gates, you will discover the most splendid gardens, fountains, and gazebos. This welcoming atmosphere then leads you into their warm and enticing lobby.

Depending on the number in your party, choose between the Bristol Room and the Grand Pavilion. The Bristol Room accommodates up to 300 people, while the Grand Pavilion seats 600 comfortably. Each ballroom has a separate entrance,

lobby, and cocktail area along with its own bridal rooms and lavatories. This ensures that your wedding is exclusive and private.

You and your guests will dine and dance the night away in surroundings that are beautiful and intimate. Each ballroom has a large marble dance floor, palladium windows, antique fireplaces, and sparkling crystal chandeliers. Both the Bristol Room and the Grand Pavilion, overlooking the softly-lit fountains of the courtyard, offer an air of romance and elegance to your evening.

At any special event, the food served is always remembered. Their chefs create culinary masterpieces that are both eye-pleasing and mouth-watering. Because their chefs each have their own area of expertise, they are able to offer you an unlimited number of options. They will design a menu that will be both distinctive and delicious.

The talents of their chefs will be evident from the start. The dining experience you have will be unique and extraordinary. Many of their chefs are graduates of the prestigious Culinary Institute of America. Savor the many different delicacies on display during the cocktail hour; you and your guests are sure to admire and enjoy them. To complement the elegance they use only the finest table accessories–Royal Doulton dinnerware and exquisite cut crystal stemware.

They are known for their custom designed menus. Their skilled staff will work with you to offer everyone at your event a first class meal.

They have their own Kosher kitchen on the premises with certified rabbinical supervision. Other ethnic menus, such as Glatt Kosher or Indian are provided with outside caterers.

The bar/bat mitzvah is a joyous celebration for your family and friends. The Rockleigh is the perfect place to commemorate your child's years of preparation and rite of passage into adulthood. They can make your son or daughter's day original and dynamic. And, to guarantee your event is hassle-free, their professional staff is ready to accommodate your every need.

There are three romantic settings to choose from for your wedding ceremony. The chapel is classically simple and can accommodate up to 600

Bride and groom enjoy the splendor of The Rockleigh.

people. If you prefer to be married outdoors, the lush Georgian Garden, with its antique French gazebo, is elegant and breathtaking. Or, say "I do" in the courtyard surrounded by fountains, flowers, and greenery.

Because they are known as a first-rate facility for weddings and bar/bat mitzvahs, The Rockleigh has the expertise and experience to host any special occasion. Their social clients celebrate anniversaries, birthdays, sweet 16's, retirement parties, bridal and baby showers and engagement parties throughout the year. And the larger dimensions of the Grand Pavilion offer an elegant setting for fashion shows,

Pan seared sea scallops with a plantain ring of wild field greens, endive, radicchio, cherry tomatoes with balsamic reduction.

proms, and fund-raisers for organizations up to 800 people.

The Rockleigh is the ideal spot for corporate functions. Their beautiful mansion style décor welcomes your guests into an atmosphere of old-world charm and elegance, and their unsurpassed personal service by their professional staff leaves no detail unattended.

The many business amenities available include

ample free parking, 75,000 square feet of meeting space, meeting rooms capable of accommodating groups of 25 to 1,000, custom menus to meet all your corporate needs, excellent cuisine for executive dining for either breakfast, lunch, or dinner, and a professional and courteous wait staff and management team.

All audio and visual equipment is available on request. Hotel accommodations are within 5 miles of the facility. High speed Internet access is available, as well as versatile meeting set ups, classroom or theatre style setups, and an excellent county golf course located directly across the street for after the meeting.

The Rockleigh is located at 26 Paris Avenue in Rockleigh; conveniently located for areas including New York, New Jersey, Connecticut, Westchester, and Rockland County. It is 15 minutes from the George Washington and Tappan Zee Bridges. For additional information call (201) 768-7171 or visit the website www.therockleigh.net.

The Brownstone

This historic landmark brownstone located in Paterson was originally built in the early 1800s, the focal point in an expanse of rolling meadows. When purchased in 1936 by Tom and Rita Clune, it was an uninhabitable shell. Although burned out with no electricity or water, it had grand old fireplaces, a lovely brownstone exterior, and a storied past that included rumors of its part in the Underground Railroad. The Clunes lovingly renovated the brownstone, preserving the hand-hewn beams and open fireplaces. With the addition of a bar and a few tables, they opened

the Brownstone House for business. Over the years the little neighborhood bar added rooms and renovated space until it could accommodate 1,000 guests. In the late 1970's, the Clunes decided to retire and sold their dream to another Paterson family they knew who also loved the Brownstone House.

That family was the Manzo family. Under the guidance of Albert and Thomas Manzo, a new chapter of extraordinary hospitality, luxury and grace began for The Brownstone.

Every detail of the historic brownstone was carefully restored and additions made to make

Pictured at right is the vaulted glass conservatory.

Shimmering beauty of The Brownstone's interior (opposite). This lavish ballroom (above) can accommodate up to 400 guests. Below, wedding cake from The Brownstone's pastry team.

The Brownstone an ideal backdrop to host an array of events from weddings to business meetings. Until you visit The Brownstone, you cannot fully appreciate the truly unique offerings of the site.

A grand marble atrium welcomes guests, offering a glimpse of the grandeur to come. A walk up the grand staircase reveals luxurious architecture in the style of a classic Italian villa. In pictorial domes, the rich colorings of hand-painted frescos are reflected in the shimmering, gracefully shaped, chandeliers. Rooms are elegantly designed featuring plush furnishings, elegant window treatments and elaborate moldings. Works of art enhance every area of The Brownstone. Charming fireplaces welcome guests in the winter as do lush garden terraces in the summer. A lavish ballroom can accommodate up to 400 guests but also offers state-of-the-art presentation equipment for the business community. Another feature of The Brownstone is a vaulted glass conser-

Conservatory set up for a reception (above) and opposite, the grand staircase.

vatory that makes it possible to host a dazzling event adding the brightness and warmth of the sun by day and the romance of the moon and stars by night. The conservatory opens up to a backdrop of stone terraces, cascading fountains and picturesque gardens. Many have used both areas for their event.

The cuisine is inspired international fare created by award-winning chefs. Menus are extensive and custom services, including catering, are available. The Brownstone offers the finest wines, spirits to compliment any choice. Service is exceptional and meticulously executed by a professional staff. You only have to experience it to understand why The Brownstone is in a class of one.

The Brownstone is located at 351 West Broadway, Paterson. The phone number is (973) 595-8582 and the website is thebrownstone.com.

Bride and groom make their entrance.

Colonial Inn

The Colonial Inn has touches of traditional and classic décor in its three magnificent banquet rooms. The largest, the Washington & Atrium Grand Ballroom, impresses guests with a glass atrium and elegant crystal chandeliers. It is spacious and can accommodate up to 400 guests. The Madison Room can accommodate up to 200 guests and has an adjacent outside patio–ideal for mingling or an al fresco cocktail hour. The equally outstanding Norwood Room caters up to 150 guests.

Ceremonies can be beautifully performed indoors or out at two new sites. Cathedral ceilings distinguish the indoor ceremony room and lavish gardens surrounding the outdoor ceremony site create a romantic ambiance. Gardens on the grounds also create a colorful canvas for photo sessions.

The Guarino family is highly regarded in the food service and catering industry and has specialized in fine dining and quality cuisine for over

A peek at a wedding reception.

Washington & Atrium Grand Ballroom.

thirty years. Paul Guarino, Sr., Paul Guarino Jr., and Nicole Guarino are involved in the day-to-day operation of the business.

Today they make their mark in the industry with the Colonial Inn and with its elegantly decorated rooms and professional and courteous staff. The Colonial Inn's notoriously lavish cocktail hours, and their attention to authentic international food, have become their trademark.

The banquet staff is prepared to anticipate your every need. Their attention to detail will assure you that your affair will be flawless. From the moment your guests arrive for the elegant cocktail hour, through your exquisitely prepared meal

Owners and operators of the Colonial Inn, Paul Guarino, Jr. and Nicole Guarino, both following in their father's footsteps.

Ice sculpture serving as a martini chiller and dispensing vessel.

of either classic or international cuisine, your celebration will be "an affair to remember."

Off-premise catering is also available. Colonial Inn is located at 545 Tappan Road in Norwood, N.J. For more information, call (201) 767-1505 or visit the website www. colonialinnnj.com.

Cathedral ceiling ceremony room.

il Tulipano

*I*l Tulipano, located on Pompton Avenue in Cedar Grove, has been family-owned and operated since 1982. Gregorio Polimeni originally founded il Tulipano as an Italian restaurant with a continental

Il Tulipano's rendition of grilled salmon (above) is artistically presented and drizzled with balsamic glaze. Il Tulipano's Domenican Ballroom (left) can comfortably seat up to 350 guests.

flair, and the establishment soon developed a serious epicurean following.

The restaurant was renovated several years later to include a ballroom with the capacity to accommodate large parties and weddings. The rest is history. Today Gregorio has both sons by his side, one in sales and management and the other in the kitchen … a true family affair. "We cater to every need and take pride in providing the finest and the freshest ingredients for the best flavor," explains co-owner Gregorio Polimeni Jr.

"At il Tulipano, your guests will celebrate in an ambiance of sophistication and elegance while dining on world class Italian regional cuisine. Our chefs create dishes that are expertly prepared and artistically presented, one fabulous wedding at a time.

"Enjoy cocktail hour on the piazza, designed to capture the warmth and beauty of the Tuscan countryside. Picture perfect, our piazza features a waterfall, brick walkway and bridal gazebo surrounded by a lush landscape. In a setting reminiscent of the Mediterranean countryside, the piazza can accommodate a large celebration or provide the perfect backdrop for an intimate wedding ceremony.

"Our property features the tastefully appointed Domenican Ballroom which can comfortably seat up to 350 guests. The room opens onto a balcony which overlooks the piazza. This terrace offers your guests a scenic view and is the perfect spot for a breath of fresh air and a stretch of the legs.

"Our Tulip Terrace is perfect for a cocktail reception or 140 guests seated for dinner. This beautifully appointed room features panoramic windows and a classic grand piano.

"Whether your celebration calls for a full course dinner or a cocktail reception, our planning professionals will work with you to craft a menu that will meet your needs and exceed your expectations."

Il Tulipano is located at 1131 Pompton Ave (Route 23) in Cedar Grove. For a complimentary consultation and tour call (973) 256-7755. Their website gives a mouthwatering in-depth look at menu possibilities for celebrating several types of occasions. Visit www.iltulipano.com.

The piazza features a waterfall, brick walkway, and bridal gazebo.

Jasna Polana

Jasna Polana can take your breath away. Its architecture, formal gardens, and expansive vistas are pure beauty. Jasna Polana is an exquisite mansion on a 230-acre estate located in Princeton, New Jersey. It was built between 1972 and 1976 as the country home of J. Seward Johnson and his wife, Barbara Piasecka Johnson. It was designed by world-renowned architect Wallace Harrison (Rockefeller Center, the Metropolitan Opera House, and the United Nations Building) to resemble a neoclassical Italian villa. The name, *Jasna Polana*, means "bright meadow" in Polish, the native language of Mrs. Johnson. Incidentally, there was a mansion owned in Moscow by Leo Tolstoy of the same name in Russia.

J. Seward Johnson was born in 1895, one of two sons of Robert Wood Johnson. His brother was Robert Wood Johnson II, the founder of the Robert Wood Johnson Foundation, a world class medical institution. The elder Robert was the president and CEO of Johnson and Johnson, Inc., the pharmaceutical giant founded by his two brothers, the original Johnson and Johnson. At RWJ Sr.'s death in 1910 the two sons inherited 87% of the company. Both were lifelong philanthropists. Seward Johnson gave millions over the years to various charities and foundations and supported many great causes such as the Solidarity movement in Poland.

Seward Johnson passed away in 1983 leaving his widow, Barbara Johnson, the current owner of the estate. She is a very intelligent and resourceful woman. Among other things, she received a master's degree in art history and an art scholarship from the Vatican, and she speaks five languages. She is known throughout the art world as a very successful art collector. Her personal collection includes works from Bellini, Rembrandt, Botticelli, Van Gogh, Gaugin, Cezanne, and Monet.

The Clubhouse is indeed an impressive sight. The stone covering the exterior is Laurel Hill sandstone quarried near Scranton, Pennsylva-

On both pages are glimpses of the 230 acres that is Jasna Polana.

nia. Each piece was "hand-dressed," that is, cut and shaped with hammer and chisel – no saws allowed. The color of the stones had to be from a particular range of colors, blue and gray shades were rejected, and the result is a beautiful salmon-hued facade. Additionally, the roof was made from 24,000 square feet of hand-sawed English slate, surrounding six tons of copper domes and gutters imported from Germany.

In 1998 Jasna Polana was opened as a private members golf club using the mansion as its clubhouse. Inside, the mansion is 46,000 square feet and holds dozens of beautiful paintings and antiques. Following is a room by room description of some highlights.

The Living Room is appointed with neo-classical furniture (Danish, Russian, Swedish, Italian, and German) from the 18th and 19th centuries. The paintings are 19th and 20thC European. The marble busts are 19thC Italian and the marble statue is 20thC Italian. The in-laid marble chimneypiece around the fireplace is 18thC French.

The Grand Foyer has two 18thC French rococo limestone chimneypieces, a large staircase made from Italian Travertine marble and several 18thC Dutch and French paintings. At the top of the first set of stairs is an 18thC French terracotta sculpture of an eagle perched on a Louis XVI marble column. The giltwood chairs around the foyer are period George I, circa 1705, and the two giltwood mirrors and console tables on either side of the front door are George II, circa 1740. Incidentally, the last four items are the most expensive pieces in the house. The oldest pieces in the house are nearby, the Italian bronze doorknockers on the front doors, which date from the late 1500's. The doors themselves are not antique, but were designed by Polish artisans who also designed and fashioned all the metalwork in and around the house, such as the front gate and the railings on the grand staircase. (Incidentally, many of these artisans were involved in the grand reconstruction of the castles of Poland that were destroyed in World War II.) Under the staircase is a George III mahogany pianoforte, the forerunner of the piano. The bronze portrait busts in each of the front corners are of Mr. and Mrs. Johnson. They were cast by the famous Italian sculptor Giacomo Manzu.

The Travertine Room, so named for the marble it is laid with, once housed the 72-foot black marble indoor swimming pool, but is now used as a large banquet facility which can seat up to 220 people. The travertine marble was quarried in Yugoslavia and cut to exacting specifications by master craftsmen in Italy. There is a spectacular view from this room of the reflecting pool and rose garden on one side and a view of the eighteenth green as well.

Upstairs Mrs. Johnson maintains her private New Jersey residence in one of two suites there. The other is called The Prince Albert Suite after the good friend of Mrs. Johnson, the crown monarch of Monaco. It is sometimes available as an overnight lodging. It features a large bedroom and private study as well as a spectacular bathroom with, among other things, a fourteen and a half foot Marble bathtub/Jacuzzi, a fireplace, a wet bar and a sauna.

The Wine Cellar is located below the grand foyer. No tour of the house would be complete without a visit here. Upon leaving the elevator a member's guests will be immediately impressed by the large bank-vault door that opens up to the wine cellar. Mr. Johnson was quite the enthusiastic collector of very fine wines. At one time his personal collection included sixty-six cases of Chateau Haut-Brion, among hundreds of other classic wines.

Today, the wine cellar features a large oak table suitable for private dining parties of up to ten people. The wine collection is still very impressive, including an array of wines from California, Italy and France. You may enjoy the likes of the Chateau Lafite-Rothschild and an array of other classed growths from Bordeaux, or you may select from many fine California wines, including numerous vintages

The Living Room appointed with neoclassical furniture.

of Opus One. Other wines in the cellar are from the Pacific Northwest, Spain, Portugal, Italy, Australia, New Zealand, South Africa and South America. Many fine vintage ports are also stored there, including several from the greatest years of the 20th century.

The Annex is a three-story 19th Century Georgian style mansion where the Johnsons originally lived while the main house was being built. This 12,500-square-foot residence features ten luxurious suites, a breakfast room, board room, living room, and billiard room. It is located by

The grand staircase made from Italian Travertine marble.

An area in The Grand Foyer revealing the front doors, which were designed by Polish artisans, and two giltwood mirrors and console tables on either side, which are George II, circa 1740.

the Route 206 gate.

Jasna Polana is beyond belief; certainly a fairytale setting for any event. There is one caveat to having an affair here – you must have a membership. Corporate and charter memberships give full privileges, while social memberships exclude golf privileges. Jasna Polana is located at 8 Lawrenceville Road in Princeton.

For additional information call (609) 688-0500 or visit the website www.tpcatjasnapolana.com.

33

Venetian Ballroom inspired by the fabulous palaces of Venice, Italy.

Lucien's Manor

Lucien's Manor is South Jersey's crown jewel. It is the most grandiose banquet facility in the region and in the top echelon of New Jersey's finest catering facilities. Family-owned and operated since 1898, this landmark piece of real-estate has maintained continued communal importance as a carriage stop on the Philadelphia to Atlantic City mainline, the area's first major inn and restaurant, and a venue to celebrate life's most momentous occasions.

The current owners completely renovated in 2001, making Lucien's Manor South Jersey's premier catering facility. Today, they continue over a century of tradition and success meeting and exceeding the expectations of clients.

In fact, Lucien himself, the Frenchman who pioneered fine dining and opulent celebrations at this location for many decades, would surely have admired the prestigious position the owners have given his namesake.

This family owned and operated facility is renowned for service. Their motto, "The customer comes first," is a classic and its practice earns a tremendous amount of "word of mouth" and repeat business. Visit this manor and it will be a family member who says hello and gives you a tour.

The Lucien's Manor's palatial size, lavish décor, and fine amenities set the stage for your special event. With their extensive selection of elegant rooms, you can find just the right size space for any celebration, large or small.

Alongside their building is a landscaped garden with waterfall and sitting area, perfect for photo opportunities. The entrance opens to a decorative lobby and grand staircase set under a majestic crystal chandelier. Imported tile, antique furniture, and classic artwork furnish the corridors.

Lucien's highly-experienced, professional culinary and catering staff, excellent food ac-companied by attentive service, and the elegant architecture and interior design all combine to enrich your special occasion, making it an affair your family, friends, and guests will never forget.

Whatever your size or style, you can be sure that every special event at Lucien's gets all the attention necessary to accommodate your special needs and requests. They will help turn your dream into elegance beyond your dreams!

Venetian Ballroom is their newest ballroom and was inspired by the fabulous palaces of Venice, Italy–any Venetian royalty would feel right at home. Elegance is everywhere. Anchoring one

The decorative lobby and grand staircase, opposite, set under a majestic crystal chandelier. La Grande Ballroom, below, featuring European décor.

The dedicated owners, (above from the left) Hristos Chris Kolovos, Bill Kolovos, and Manwell Baroody, who have redefined sumptuous celebrating in South Jersey. Bride and groom, above right, dance on the Venetian's inlaid dance floor. A wedding cake (opposite) from Lucien's pastry team. Bride and groom pose under Lucien's fanciful gazebo.

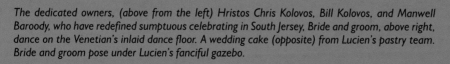

Lucien himself, the Frenchman who pioneered fine dining and opulent celebrations at this location... would have admired the prestigious position the owners have given his namesake.

corner is a beautiful fireplace. In the other, water gently cascades down a tiled wall. Around the room, beautiful marbleized columns adorned with gilded capitals stretch up to intricate cornices, which surround a hand-painted faux sky ceiling. Ornate crystal chandeliers and nine foot windows bathe the room in a warm glow. The wedding party sits upon a raised head table situated perfectly to observe their guests, and the beauty of their Venetian Room. Venetian parties enjoy a private entrance, separate kitchen, and their own guest facilities. Floor plans can be arranged to accommodate anywhere from 200-325 guests.

La Grande Ballroom is a breathtaking ballroom with European décor and a tropical indoor waterfall with gardens that change throughout the seasons. Enjoy dining with a view of their customized hand carved mantle and granite fireplace. An elevated ceiling with elegant crystal chandeliers and sconces will set your dinner ambiance to perfection. Floor plans can range from 200-550 guests.

Versailles Ballroom, a distinctively designed ballroom with a marble fireplace, Pergo dance floor, and cascading crystal chandeliers along with corresponding sconces, is an elegant venue for 150-200

guests. The room was designed with an open floor plan and balconies to observe the scenery below. The staircase from the balcony above to the main floor is perfect for your grand entrance as Husband and Wife.

Nouvelle Ballroom is the ideal setting for intimate wedding receptions. Perfect in every way, the Nouvelle is quaint but richly decorated, giving even the smallest event an elegant ambiance. This ballroom accommodates a minimum of 100 guests and a maximum of 150 guests.

The Stone Grille restaurant, owned by the same owners as Lucien's, offers special deals to bride and grooms for engagement parties, rehearsal dinners, bridal showers, and special occasions. Located at 1300 Blackwood Clementon Road in Clementon, the Stone Grille is a unique attraction. Steaks, lobsters, and other delicacies are cooked on special heated stones.

Lucien's Manor is located at 81 West White Horse Pike, Berlin. For more information call (856) 768-9444 or visit the website www.luciensmanor. com. The Stone Grille's phone number is (856) 782-7111 and additional information is available on the website www. stonegrille.com.

The Palace
at
Somerset Park

Situated on 30 tranquil wooded acres, The Palace at Somerset Park is a premier venue for exceptional weddings, galas, celebrations, productive meetings,

West Ballroom setup for a formal dinner party(left). (Above, clockwise) The captivating front exterior of The Palace. Pan seared foie gras with a walnut persimmon bread, fig jam, and sweet port wine glace. Several wedding cakes designed by The Palace's pastry chef.

41

East Ballroom.

Salon II.

dynamic conferences, and sophisticated occasions.

Corporate clients consider The Palace an executive retreat and the model of efficiency. The rooms blend practical features such as ergonomic seating, plentiful natural lighting, and individual climate controls with the elegance of couture fabrics, antique accents, and original artwork. The option of their unique exclusivity advantage guarantees groups of 350 or more the benefit of complete privacy and a distraction-free

Wok station (above) with full Asian theme. Below is the Grand Foyer.

*Above, a bride admires
a moonlit sky on the
West Terrace. At left, the
bridal suite, known as the
Somerset Library.*

Truffle-egged mousse with Sevruga caviar and chive thread.

environment for the duration of the event. From healthful refreshment breaks to inspired modern American entrees, their distinguished culinary staff has developed menus to satisfy the most discerning tastes. With The Palace's dedicated planning professionals at your service, arranging the ideal event is effortless. They invite you to view their rooms and resources, and determine how they can help you achieve brilliant results.

Upon arrival to this private estate for social events, gracious servers welcome guests with champagne flutes and the promise of an unforgettable occasion. Enjoy magnificent ballrooms with Juliet balconies, luxurious suites, grand terraces with garden views, and exquisite touches, such as marble fireplaces, antique fountains, and crystal chandeliers. Their renowned culinary team prepares inventive creations to suit every taste. Kosher and Indian cuisine can be arranged through

their preferred partners. Discreetly installed audiovisual technology maintained by expert IT technicians integrates function with style. Advanced LCD projectors, sound systems, and cable and wireless high-speed internet access keep your event looking and sounding superb. The attentive care of their dedicated planning professionals ensures a flawless event for your guests and effortless planning for you.

The Palace is centrally located and easily accessible from Morristown, Parsippany, New Brunswick, Princeton, and just 45 minutes from Manhattan and 30 minutes from Newark International Airport. The Palace offers 44,000 square feet of purpose-built meeting space accommodating groups up to 1,000. An array of versatile rooms can be configured to your group's preference. Call (732) 302-9922 or visit the website www.palacesomersetpark.com for additional information.

45

Pergola and dancing water.

South Gate Manor

With over 25 years of professional catering experience, the Marino family has dedicated themselves to a continuous tradition of catering excellence and personal attention. The newly redesigned and exquisitely decorated South Gate Manor is adorned with rich mahogany woodwork, fine alabaster lighting, elegant granite, and an outdoor pavilion designed for cocktail receptions.

South Gate Manor offers impressive spaces for each phase of your celebration. The entrance opens to a sweeping staircase, sky dome, and player piano. A high ceiling and spacious corridor appointed with beautiful drapery leads guests to other destinations throughout the facility. The cocktail room draws attention with its thousand light dome and "alfresco ambiance." A large bridal suite with full bar and food service is beautifully furnished and features a flat screen TV for live viewing of the cocktail room. The lofty ceiling of the ballroom flaunts large alabaster light fixtures and mahogany detail. The newly completed outdoor garden offers a pristine ceremony setting. Geyser fountains with dancing waters surround a perched pergola. On special request, brides may have their flower of choice planted in the beds surrounding the site for the day of their affair and an in-house florist is available.

South Gate Manor's specialty is customizing each wedding to the couple. They offer an outstanding cocktail hour, impressive dinner menu choices, and an over-the-top dessert display.

Enjoy white glove service, valet parking, and rest room attendants. The professional and courteous staff of South Gate Manor await to fulfill your guests' every need. The South Gate Manor is located at 260 South Street in Freehold. For information call (732) 431-1500 or visit www.southgatemanornj.com.

The cocktail room and its light accented dome.

The Westwood

estled in the quaint town of Garwood, The Westwood has long been exceeding the expectations of their wedding couples and corporate clients. The Westwood, known for fabulous food and impeccable service, offers their guests unparalleled amenities in an inviting and elegant atmosphere. A beautifully appointed ballroom, sets the stage for a once in a lifetime event. An indoor garden room is perfect for ceremonies and picture taking.

Family owned since 1961, The Westwood is often catering weddings for children and even grandchildren of past brides and grooms. The staff often have their own affairs at The Westwood—a true testament to quality and consistency. Over 45 years of doing business has by no means instilled any complacency. The Westwood continues to keep up with the times–remodeling, re-inventing. The Westwood is a member of several catering associations. Both management and staff attend seminars–keeping up with what's new in the industry and utilizing current trends at their affairs.

Enjoy white glove service and the pampering of well trained maitre d's and captains. Executive Chef Tim Jones, a 21 year veteran of The Westwood, is a Johnson and Whales Culinary school graduate. His repertoire includes magnificent custom ice sculptures. Bring in a picture and he will replicate it in shimmering ice. Enjoy exquisite desserts; all baking is done on premise by an in-house pastry chef. The Westwood has several wedding packages to choose from or will create your own personal menu customizing your special day to your specific tastes.

The Westwood also handles many corporate events, everything from breakfast meetings and luncheons to all day conferences with theme breaks and theme buffets as refreshers. In-house audiovisual equipment is available for presentations.

All the frills of an elegant table setting; The Westwood has assorted linens and candelabras from which to create your desired décor. Bride and groom and fine architectural details at The Westwood.

The elegantly appointed Cynthia Ballroom.

The Westwood is known for affordability and consistency. All social and business affairs are hosted, including weddings, bar mitzvahs, bat mitzvahs, corporate events, fundraisers, sweet 16's, communions, showers, reunions, and christenings. Events range in size from 50 to 500 people. Off-premise catering is also available and ranges from an intimate gathering of 20 to a full service catered affair of 5000. The Westwood is located at 438 North Avenue in Garwood. Let The Westwood exceed your expectations by calling (908) 789-0808 or visit the website www.thewestwood.com.

Chef Tim Jones, a 21-year veteran of The Westwood, flambéing a dessert and several of his culinary creations. Clockwise from top right: Cheesecake presented with fresh fruit, raspberry sorbet—usually served as a colorful intermezzo, bruchetta, and detailed ice carving of a swan.

53

Chapter 2
With a View

The Hyatt Regency in Jersey City and the breathtaking New York skyline view.

Lobby view.

Hyatt Regency
Jersey City

The Hyatt Regency promises a new level of luxury in Jersey City. Located on the harbor side Financial Center's south pier overlooking Manhattan, the hotel is directly across from Wall Street. Achieving new standards in hospitality, the hotel offers corporate and social catering, an exceptional dining experience at Vu restaurant, modern surroundings, and elegant guest accommodations, many with breathtaking views.

Hyatt Regency Jersey City was designed to accommodate meetings and conferences of all sizes in style and comfort. The hotel features state-of-the-art meeting amenities, including high-speed Internet access and high-tech lighting and sound systems. The hotel's third floor has 20,000 square feet of functions space, including the 7,691 square foot Hudson Ballroom; the 6,500 square foot Manhattan Ballroom, with spectacular Manhattan skyline views and a spacious outdoor terrace; the Riverview Boardroom; and an additional 6,000 square feet of self-contained conference space. The hotel is well-suited for business retreats or private social events.

Vu restaurant features an innovative, contemporary menu highlighting fine steaks and fish. Savor American cuisine as you gaze out at the Hudson River and Statue of

Hyatt Regency and the Jersey City financial district.

Liberty. The incomparable New York City skyline is your dining partner at Vu. Whether you are beginning your day with a hearty breakfast or celebrating over dinner, you'll enjoy a feast for your eyes as well as your taste buds. The talented chefs of this Jersey City restaurant craft a seasonal menu designed to complement this astounding backdrop. How about pan seared foie gras with caramelized figs, port reduction, fleur de sel, and ground coffee beans; flounder and crab Napoleon with chervil cream sauce and grilled Mediterranean vegetables; and pan seared elk strip steak with prosciutto gnocchi and creamy cabbage and cranberry compote.

Also enjoy Vu Lounge. A favorite of guests and locals alike, this elegant Jersey City bar offers stunning views, refreshing cocktails, and tempting light fare. Visit Vu Lounge for a fast, light lunch, beginning your night with a drink, winding down with a nightcap, or to gaze at the city lights shining over the Hudson River.

The Hyatt Regency is located at 2 Exchange Place in Jersey City. The hotel is conveniently located just 15 minutes from Newark International Airport and a quick ferry or PATH train ride to lower Manhattan, midtown shops, theatre district, and museums. There are 350 guestrooms and 13 suites with views of the Manhattan skyline. For additional information call (201) 469-4745 or visit the website www.jerseycity.hyatt.com.

Adventure Aquarium

Conveniently located on the Camden Waterfront, just two miles from Center City Philadelphia, Adventure Aquarium offers a unique setting for corporate and social events. Take in scenic views of the Philadelphia skyline while wandering through exotic and fascinating exhibits. Mingle in front of the 760,000-gallon Ocean Realm exhibit full of colorful fish, turtles, and stingrays while enjoying cocktails and hors d'oeuvres.

The 40 foot walk-through tunnel (above) completely surrounded by water, part of Shark Realm, is set for guests. Table setting (right) in a large viewing area of Shark Realm.

Dive into even more excitement with an excursion into the all new North building. Thrill your guests with a walk through the West African River Experience, featuring hippopotamuses, porcupines, more than 1,000 fish, and free-flight aviary. For an up close encounter, venture into the Shark Realm through the 40 foot walk-through tunnel completely surrounded by water. You'll explore the unknown as you travel into a beautiful, bizarre, and wondrous deep sea world. Adventure Aquarium offers your guests a one-of-a-kind experience.

Adventure Aquarium is available for private events after five o'clock when the facility closes to the general public. This venue has been used for meetings, holiday parties, weddings, bar and bat mitzvahs, proms and galas. The exotic Jules Verne Gallery and captivating Shark Realm are thrilling areas to host a private dinner or cocktail party. Guests can also experience the Aquarium by dining and dancing in the Rotunda under warm lighting and a spectacular iridescent fish mobile.

Professional event planners are available to guide you through the many options on how the facilities can be used for your event. Possibilities include Underwater Journey–guests enjoy Irazu Falls, Caribbean Currents, and Ocean Realm. Capacities are 1,500 for cocktails and hors d'oeuvres, 350 for sit down, and 750 for buffet. Underwater Safari–guests enjoy: Shark Realm, West African River Experience, and Jules Verne Gallery featuring Japanese giant spider crabs, leafy and weedy sea dragons, sea nettles, an octopus, and much more. Capacities are 200 for cocktails and hors d'oeuvres, 350 for sit down, and 500 for buffet.

The Open Ocean Voyage is a total aquarium option. Guests can have a wonderful cocktail reception while viewing all the exhibits, and then sit down for dinner in front of the Ocean Realm viewing window with views of magnificent fish from around the world.

Guests enjoy Irazu Falls, Caribbean Currents, Ocean Realm, Coral Cove, Creature Lab, Shark Realm, West African River Experience, and Jules Verne Gallery.

Capacities are 3,000 for cocktails and hors d'oeuvres, 350 for sit down, and 1,000 for buffet. Additional options allow for including the dive show, touch-a-shark tank, 4D theater, and seal

Ceremony taking place and Ocean Realm is the backdrop.

Guests admire the sea live as a party is in full swing.

and penguin shows. For smaller, daytime events they offer two rooms for presentations, breakfasts, or luncheons. The Skyline Room and Rotunda Annex can seat from 60 to 120 guests.

The exclusive in-house caterer, Aramark, takes great pride in providing fabulous cuisine. Their creative culinary team presents memorable dining experiences, from formal dinners and receptions to casual buffets. Their catering sales professional can customize a menu to suit your individual tastes.

Adventure Aquarium is located at 1 Aquarium Drive at the Delaware River Waterfront in Camden – opposite Penn's Landing in Philadelphia and just minutes from the Ben Franklin Bridge, I-676, I-295 and New Jersey Turnpike. For more information contact the facility sales office at (856) 365-3300 or visit the website www.adventureaquarium.com.

Avalon Yacht Club

Rebuilt in 1998, the Avalon Yacht Club has been one of the Jersey Shore's most breathtaking private clubs since 1941. With every view clearly overlooking the water, the Avalon Yacht Club makes an ideal location to hold your wedding.

Weddings are hosted during the spring and fall seasons, but unfortunately not in the summer months between Memorial Day and Labor Day, when the club is in season. At the Avalon Yacht Club a well seasoned staff caters to your every need, whether you have a large, extravagant wedding or a small, intimate reception. When you have your sponsored wedding at the Avalon Yacht Club, the entire building is reserved for you and your guests. You won't spend just your wedding day at the Avalon Yacht Club; membership for a year is included in the wedding package so you will be able to enjoy the atmosphere for more than just your special day. Wedding ceremonies can take place in front of a magnificent view on the north deck, weather permitting. Otherwise, the ceremony can be held on an indoor balcony.

Terry Thompson, the onsite event manager, will gladly coordinate all planning and details for your wedding. Terry has been the general manager for the Avalon Yacht Club for the past 10 years. She will assist you in getting the perfect floral arrangement, best entertainment, wedding cake of any kind, favors, and every intricate detail to make your wedding day everything you dreamed. Terry will also help you coordinate your day around the exact time of sunset, to ensure beautiful wedding pictures with the best background nature can provide. According to

Philadelphia Magazine Best of the Shore 2006, the Avalon Yacht Club was rated best of the shore for wedding sunsets.

Peter Mark, the executive chef of the Avalon Yacht Club for 18 years, will provide the cuisine for your special day. From a one entree dinner, to a choice of three, Chef Peter will work with you one on one to figure out which foods will best cater to you and your guests.

During the summer months the club is in full swing with a variety of activities to suite every age. The Youth and Sailing program is one of the largest on the east coast. Children of all ages sail their sunfishes' out on the bay, closely monitored by the excellent staff of the program. "Deck Parties" are very common around the club. In the summer months live bands perform outside on the deck.

The dining room offers exceptional food prepared by highly trained chefs. The club's menu consists of the freshest locally caught seafood including scallops, flounder, clams, crab cakes, and much more. If seafood doesn't delight your palate, the chefs also prepare the most succulent filet mignon, chicken, veal, and more.

The Avalon Yacht Club is located at 704 7th Street in Avalon. Visit their website for further information, as well as membership information, at www.avalonyachtclub.com. The Avalon Yacht Club can be reached at (609) 967-4444.

From the left, a table setting just before guests' arrival. Onsite Event Manager Terry Thompson and Executive Chef Peter Mark. Here the club is set up for an elegant reception. Background and inset pictures are examples of the breathtaking view.

Classic cocktails, dining with a view, and fine wines are all part of the Bateaux experience.

Bateaux

*I*nspired by the glass-enclosed vessels of Europe, Bateaux is truly a gourmet experience in a setting unlike any other. Bateaux was featured as the site of NBC's Today Show wedding reception in 2003. This vessel is the only glass dining yacht sailing the Hudson. It is an intimate venue for two to 300 guests. Semi-private charters are available in the Aurora Room for one-hundred-seventy guests and in the Orion Room for one-hundred-thirty guests. Bateaux is an exceptional choice for entertaining with an exclusive sense of style.

The magnificent New York skyline spreads before you in all directions. You will be pampered with gourmet cuisine, fine wines, live jazz, and sophisticated dance music on this amazing dining cruise. Bateaux cruises the Hudson and East Rivers past skyscrapers of Manhattan, providing you with a breathtaking view of some of the world's most celebrated landmarks, including the Brooklyn Bridge, Statue of Liberty, and Ellis Island.

Aboard the Bateaux the glass ceiling and walls reveal a magnificent view, while rich hardwood floors gleam underfoot. World-class entertainment features songs inspired by the sights surrounding you, and Bateaux's exceptional service standards ensure that the night is pure perfection.

Bateaux is all class. Climate-controlled comfort is enhanced by a ceiling shade system. There is a spacious hardwood dance floor and a revolutionary deck layout gives every person's table a view of the entertainment. A state-of-the-art sound system has speakers that customize volume levels. Bateaux's extensive wine cellar maintains select wines in a temperature-controlled environment. Two outdoor decks allow open air enjoyment.

Bateaux can leave from Lincoln Harbor Marina in Weehawken or across the Hudson at the Chelsea Piers. Special cruises include Easter Sunday dinner cruise, Mother's Day cruises, Father's Day cruise, and the 4th of July Fireworks cruise. For additional information call 1-866-211-3806 or visit the website www.bateauxnewyork.com.

Lake Mohawk
Country Club

Lake Mohawk is a homeowners association featuring a village square much like those tucked away in the Swiss Alps. The highlight of the experience is the Lake Mohawk Country Club Clubhouse, designed reminiscent of a Swiss castle with peaks, spires, and balconies centered on a beautifully landscaped boardwalk complete with a beach and overlooking breathtaking views of the lake nestled into the colorful foothills of Northern New Jersey.

A private bridal suite can be yours with a three story tower view of the cascading hills and magnificent homes adorning the lake. The bridal suite comes complete with private dressing area, a lounging area, bar, and private intimate hors d'oeuvres presentation. Nearby in the lake community are many magnificent salons and day spas prepared to pamper you while doing hair, nails, and massage therapy. The total experience allows you to start your day with a complete makeover, dress on location, and take those most precious pictures stress free before the guests arrive.

Cocktail hour on the Boardwalk (above). Bridal suite view of on going cocktail hour (left).

–Photographs courtesy of
  D. Becker Photo.

Lake Mohawk Country Club provides both outdoor lakeside ceremony and cocktail hour settings on the boardwalk, or an indoor opportunity with a lake view. Lake Mohawk Country Club, as stated by the Chamber of Commerce, is "New Jersey's best kept secret." Established in 1929, the Clubhouse is on the National Register and the New Jersey Register of Historic Landmarks.

It has been masterfully enhanced by Frances Smith, General Manager, since 1985. The on-site Wedding Consultant and Planner, Larry Patton, has networked with the finest in wedding services since 1990. This includes ceremony officiants, florists, entertainment, salons, bridal specialists, and hotels or stately bed and breakfasts. The renowned Lake Mohawk Country

A collage of the Lake Mohawk Country Club experience.

– Photographs courtesy of D. Becker Photo.

71

Club has been the selected and
talked about site for hundreds of weddings, family gatherings, and very special social events, as Larry and his seasoned staff
orchestrate formal dinners, beach parties, or cruise liner presentation buffets.
The Executive Chef since 1995, Jacobo Dominguez, accentuates the wonderful
culinary experience with his staff to provide international cuisine and award-winning
ice sculpture artistry.
The Grand Ballroom is truly a Grand Ballroom with a gorgeous Maplewood floor spanning
the entire 4,000 square foot room featuring a Palladian window overlooking the lake. Crystal
Victorian chandeliers adorn the cathedral ceiling and the rich, beautiful window treatments
complete a truly fairy tale dream come true experience.
Lake Mohawk Country Club is located at 21 The Boardwalk in Sparta. You can contact
Lake Mohawk Country Club by phone at (973) 729-6156, by e-mail using www.
catering@lakemohawkcountryclub.com, or just visit the website
www.lakemohawkcountryclub.com.

A peek into the Grand Ballroom (left). Picture perfect ending at Lake Mohawk Country Club (above). Photographs courtesy of D

Newark Club

$\mathcal{W}$elcome to the Newark Club—one of New Jersey's most elegant venues for special celebrations. Located in the heart of Newark's downtown renaissance, The Club features breathtaking panoramic views for miles around. The magnificence outside is matched by the elegance inside. Upon arrival you will be greeted by sophistication, comfort, and graciousness, evident throughout the stylishly luxurious décor.

Weddings are personalized events that are expressions of your style and individuality. With this in mind, their expert staff of event professionals will assist you in creating the celebration of your dreams, artfully employing the best traditions of service, hospitality, and friendliness to ensure that all of the details converge to create a flawless experience.

A wedding is a time-honored celebration of two lives joining as one. Your wedding venue should be a reflection of your dreams and aspirations as you embark on life's journey together. The most discerning couples will find this stunning venue to be a perfect platform from which to launch a life of love and attachment.

The staff members of Newark Club.

Catering manager, Harry Prott, puts the finishing touch on a wedding cake.

Antique estate silver and radiant candelabras embellish a warm patina of elegant splendor as your guests are greeted by friendly faces bearing the signature silver champagne service and lavish trays of hors d'oeuvres and canapés.

Chef Peter Parello and his team of culinary artists strive to make each catered experience uniquely satisfying. The hand crafted menus feature imaginative and original cuisine utilizing only the freshest, highest quality ingredients prepared perfectly and served in beautifully artistic presentations.

Weddings, bar mitzvahs, anniversaries, reunions, or birthday parties... no matter your

22nd floor— Newark Club (left). Assortment of desserts for after dinner indulgence (right).

Chef Peter Parello (above) applies a demi-glaze. Ashmore Thomas (above right), a 15 year veteran of Newark Club.

special occasion, the Newark Club can provide the ideal setting. From an intimate cocktail party to an elaborate dinner, you can be assured that your every expectation will be surpassed. Their elegant surroundings can be arranged to reflect the theme, ambiance, and size of your event. Whether an intimate gathering or an extrava-gant gala, you will find the Newark Club to be exceptional and remarkable.

The Newark Club is located on the 22nd Floor at One Newark Center in Newark. For additional information call (973) 242.0658 or visit the website www.newarkclub.com.

One of the staff mobilizes a silver platter of assorted cheeses and fresh fruit. Champagne glasses (right) being garnished with fresh strawberries.

Perona Farms

Perona Farms was Emil Perona's American dream. His career began in the kitchen of a London hotel at the age of fourteen, progressed to vaudeville stages all over the world, and culminated in 1917 with the purchase of a 260 acre dairy farm in Andover, where he planned to lead the unassuming life of a dairy farmer with his wife, Angiolina.

However, Emil's income did not keep pace with the appetites of his cows. He decided to take in boarders to offset expenses. Emil's brother, John, owner of the famous New York restaurant and Nightclub, the El Morocco, helped by sending his party-weary customers to the country for rest and relaxation. The scenic country atmosphere, along with Angiolina's cooking, made Perona Farms the retreat of choice.

Word spread and the farmhouse table could no longer accommodate the multitude of eager diners. The evolution from farm to boardinghouse to restaurant to premier wedding site was a response to customers' desires. Customer satisfaction and culinary distinction still secure Perona Farms' reputation as one of New Jersey's most beautifully idyllic wedding and banquet facilities.

No longer a farmhouse, the restaurant resembles a sprawling Mediterranean villa resplendent with its subtle elegance. The grounds are romantically inviting and meticulously landscaped. Guests still enjoy the stroll across Emil's handcrafted bridge to the little island on Perona Lake.

Today, Mark, Wade, Kirk and Tracey, the great-grandchildren of Emil and Angiolina Perona, continue the family tradition of hospitality and excellence. With the help of over 100 associates, they remain committed to maintaining the highest standards of fine cuisine and service.

Bride and Groom on Emil Perona's handcrafted bridge that leads to the little island on Perona Lake.

Guests enjoy private patios, courtyards, and terraces where ceremonies and cocktail parties abound al fresco. Each event is secluded with its own entrance, bridal room, crystal chandelier-lit ballroom, outdoor cocktail area and restrooms. The chefs, banquet department, and maitre d's all work together to ensure every event exceeds the guests' expectations. Nothing is overlooked except the countryside.

In addition to its renowned weddings and banquets, Perona Farms has been serving its sumptuous Sunday "Bruncheon" since 1974 and crafting its World's #1 Rated Smoked Salmon since 1992. Perona Farms also provides off premises catering and takeout to serve the needs of its customers at home or at work.

Perona Farms started in 1917 around the boardinghouse table. The food was exceptional, the conversation lively, and the hosts hospitable. Almost a century later, little has changed – family traditions remain.

Perona Farms is located at 350 Andover-Sparta Road (Route 517) in Andover, approximately 65 miles Northwest of New York City. Explore Perona Farms in detail at www.peronafarms.com, or call (973) 729-6161.

Courtyard party in full swing.

Kirk Avondoglio

Executive Chef Kirk Avondoglio is an exciting contemporary chef who is sought after from his home state's Drumthwacket, the official home of the New Jersey Governor in Princeton, to California, the Far East, and Brazil. He participated in the First Festival of Master Chefs, held at the Intercontinental Hotel in Mexico City and has given several seminars at Columbus Isle in The Bahamas for Club Med Resorts.

He has been recognized by Art Culinare, the James Beard Society, The New York Times, New York Newsday, Asbury Park Press, and the Chicago Tribune as one of America's top contemporary chefs.

Kirk has hosted James Beard Dinners and has cooked at The James Beard House in New York City on many occasions. He has also appeared on "Ready, Set, Cook" on TV's Food Network Cable Channel.

After trying his hand at smoking salmon in his great-grandfather's smokehouse, Kirk and his siblings established Perona Farms Food Specialties in 1992.

Since that time, Cook's Illustrated Magazine has rated his smoked salmon the number one smoked salmon in the world. It is now shipped worldwide to the finer hotels, restaurants, and to discerning chefs.

Pictured at right is a banquet room and several romantic views of brides and grooms at Perona Farms.

The grand ballroom (above) accommodates seating for 150 people and overlooks the golf course. Below a bride and groom pose beneath a stone archway which leads to the ceremony site.

Ramsey Golf & Country Club

Ramsey Golf & Country Club has been a treasured location for social and corporate affairs. A reputation for magnificent cuisine, impeccable service, and breathtaking views brings both corporate planners and brides to this captivating destina-tion. Weddings are celebrated one at a time at Ramsey Golf & Country Club. A castle tucked among formal gardens, lakes, and trees makes the perfect setting for your day whether you envision a romantic fairy tale or an elegant affair uniquely your own.

The present club had its beginning in the early 1900s as a 220- acre estate called "Arlena Towers," which was carefully developed over a 30

year period by its two owners. The original man-sion was of ancient Norman architecture and was modeled after the famous Ramsey Abbey, which still stands in Hampshire, Country of Hants, England and was erected by King Edward the Elder about 900 A.D. Many of the materials for the mansion were im-ported from England to add to the structural authenticity and charm.

The elaborate landscaping, plant-ings, and seedlings of the estate were begun by the original owner, Arthur Brandeis of department store and theatrical fame. The beautification of the property was completed by the second owner, Jo-seph DeWyckoff, co-founder of the Vanadium Corp. of America. Three

acre seeded lawn, now part of the golf course, was considered the largest and best-kept lawn in the East. Around 1935, "Arlena Towers" was awarded first prize as the most beautiful estate in America in the National Better Lawns and Gardens contest.

In 1940, the DeWyckoff Estate was sold to National House & Farms Association for residential development and was named the Ramsey Country Club Estates. Each individual purchaser, by accepting a title, agreed to abide by the rules of the club and was issued a share of stock–a practice that continues to this day. The starting price of a home at that time was approximately $5,000.

Approximately 40 homes were completed before material shortages due to World War II forced construction to a halt. Being unable to continue with construction, National House & Farms offered the remaining lots for sale and agreed to turn over the mansion and surround-

Chick Callahan demonstrates the art of making a Bloody Mary, a skill he has perfected for more than fifty years at Ramsey Golf and Country Club. Tenure, although not as long as Chick's, is high amongst the staff at Ramsey Golf & Country Club and contributes to the professionalism and impeccable service guests receive at this cherished establishment.

beautiful lakes were developed on the property, the largest Crystal Lake, covering 30 acres. Their shaded banks were landscaped and planted and the mansion was surrounded by towering trees and beautiful gardens. Hundreds of varieties of trees, shrubs, and flowers abounded, many of which were imported and very rare for this area. The 50

ing property, including the original golf course, to the existing homeowners. Thus, the Ramsey Golf and Country Club was born. The early members dedicated many hours of their time and labor toward the maintenance and improvement of the grounds and facilities. At that time, there was no staff of any kind, so all cooking, serving, cleaning,

Ceremony site overlooks a manicured fairway.

and gardening was done by the members.

In 1953, the membership initiated a series of improvements, which included doubling the size of the original ballroom, adding the patio, and filling in the sunken gardens to provide a parking lot. In 1961, a capital assessment was approved to finance further major improvements and the purchase of an additional 17 acres of land to increase the size of the golf course. Much later, the bowling alley was converted into what is currently the Pro-Shop. The Platform Tennis Courts, which are located behind the Pro-Shop, were introduced to the club in 1978.

Further renovation had been approved to enlarge the kitchen and to update the ballroom and Grille Room facilities when a disastrous fire occurred on February 14, 1986. The fire left the building completely gutted. All that remained was the original stonewalls. What originally had been renovation plans were quickly converted to reconstruction plans. It was decided that the original stonewalls would be preserved, and 17 months later the Clubhouse was completely and authentically restored and enlarged by 8,000 square feet. The new structure accommodated a grand ballroom, seating 150 people, the Abbey's formal dining area, a private dining room, and The Grille Room, the terrace, and office facilities located on the third floor. The reopening of the Clubhouse was celebrated on August 1, 1987 with a flag raising, ribbon cutting ceremony, and a champagne brunch. In addition, nearly 400 club members attended a dinner and dance in celebration of the Clubhouse's reopening. On July 2, 1995, after many years of planning and two years of construction to the existing course, the Ramsey Golf & Country Club officially opened its 18 holes.

Ramsey Golf & Country Club is located at 105 Lakeside Drive in Ramsey. For additional information or to tour the club, call (201) 327-0009 or visit the website www.ramseycountryclub.com.

Ravello

Ravello, a Tuscan villa set amidst an elegant and serene setting, could easily be in Florence or Rome–for it's truly a world-class establishment in the image of Italy's finest. Conceived and directed by the Venturi family, Ravello has quickly emerged to become one New Jersey's premiere wedding and event venues.

With more than thirty-five years experience in the hospitality industry, the Venturi family has achieved a stellar reputation for both exceptional cuisine and gracious service. Hosting only one wedding at a time, Ravello promises a day that is uniquely the bride and groom's. The lush gardens, romantic fountains, and charming gazebo create an atmosphere of pure elegance from the moment you arrive, and offer the ideal setting for a picture perfect on-site ceremony. The tastefully appointed bridal suite and magnificent grand ballroom com-

Veranda view of the grounds (top). Classic white wedding cake (left) by Ravello. Waterfall pond (below left). Festive celebration at Ravello (below and center, opposite).

plete the picture. Superb cuisine, artistic presentations, and the gracious hospitality of an attentive, white-gloved staff will enchant your guests and ensure memories to last a lifetime. Each detail is flawlessly crafted to create the magical event every couple deserves.

Ravello is also pleased to offer social and corporate event planning for any size and occasion. From sales conferences to fundraisers, engagement parties to sweet sixteen celebrations, they specialize in customized and unique events for every occasion and budget.

Ravello has recently announced the opening of their off-premise catering division to serve your needs at home or at the office, covering a small order for pick-up to a lunch or dinner party complete with food, beverage, staff, and rentals.

Ravello is a family owned and operated facility; the complete satisfaction of their valued clientele is always their utmost priority. Contact Ravello at (973) 781-9001 to make an appointment for a personal tour of their villa. They are gracious and always look forward to welcoming you. Ravello is located at 138 Eagle Rock Avenue in East Hanover. Additional information can be found on the website www.ravellobanquets.com.

Multi-level Gothic lion headed fountain (above right).
Ravello's picturesque gazebo (right).

Photographs courtesy of Morello Entertainment.

Renault Winery Resort & Golf

Tuscany House (opposite). (Above) Grand foyer and ballroom of Tuscany House.

Dual pools of Tuscany House (above) which often is used for a ceremony site.

enault Winery Resort and Golf is ideal for all types of social and corporate affairs and offers a world of activities to complement your event. You can have a great dinner, stay over, have brunch the next day, play a round of golf, listen to entertainment, tour the winery and taste the wines, and much more. It is in fact, the largest destination resort outside Atlantic City. 1,400 acres of vineyards, gardens, fairways, and streams make up the renowned Renault.

The Renault Winery has been producing its exceptional wines since 1864, when Louis Renault journeyed from Reims, France. Nearly a century and a half old, Renault Winery is a recognized New Jersey state historical site and one of the oldest continuously operating vineyards in the United States.

Take an interesting tour and learn the unique history of Renault Winery and its founder. It begins in The Fountain Room and continues on to the celebrated Antique Glass Museum which houses a priceless champagne and wine glass collection

Joseph's Restaurant's Romaine hearts served with creamy parmesan dressing, topped with focaccia croutons and parmesan chards.

dating back to medieval times. The tour eventually concludes in the Wine Tasting Emporium where you'll have the opportunity to sample the Renault's award winning wine and champagne selections.

From high-level executive meetings to the most elegant receptions, the Renault Winery Resort & Golf meeting facilities provide an intimate and gracious ambiance for all occasions. The options for celebrations both large and small are many. The Grand Ballroom has seating for 280 and includes a staircase for the bride and groom to make their royal entrance. Cocktail hour is held magnificently in the Veranda Room equipped with a baby grand piano and windows that overlook scenic green grounds. The Vintage room is an old-world style room accented with wine casks and a working fireplace. It has a romantic ambiance and comfortably fits 60-150 people with a dance floor. There are three ceremony sites, one overlooking the golf course, one overlooking the pond, and one overlooking the pools of Joseph's Tuscany House. The Renault also offers over 10,000 square feet of flexible meeting space,

Joseph's Restaurant's Seafood Martini (right) filled with chilled jumbo shrimp, lump crabmeat and served with a duo of sauces. (Below) Golf course view.

Mural covered wall in the Tuscany house courtyard (above). Barrel with Louis Renault depiction decorating the grounds of Renault Winery (below).

including high speed internet access and state-of-the art audio visual equipment.

In addition, the resort also features two award-winning restaurants led by accomplished chefs. Dinner at the gourmet restaurant at Renault is an event to remember. The innovative menu invites guests to choose one of 8 exquisitely prepared entrees, while the executive chef complements their meals with the evening's special appetizer, homemade soup, pasta, ice-cold sorbet intermezzo, gourmet salad, and two wine samplings, adding an element of adventure and surprise. Also enjoy live music and dancing. Join them Sunday mornings for their award-winning brunch.

Joseph's Restaurant within the Tuscany House is a place to relax, indulge, and experience old world luxury. Executive Chef Joseph Degennero prepares an extraordinary menu unique to South Jersey. Start your evening off with a home-made appetizer or fresh salad. All steaks are certified Angus beef. Joseph's features entrees such as Veal Napoleon, Delmonico Steaks, Seafood paella, and luscious pasta dishes. Live piano music is featured on the weekends.

The Tuscany house at the Renault Winery allows for overnight stays and is reminiscent of an Italian villa. Fine European furnishings, two swimming pools, verandas, and a lovely courtyard distinguish this establishment.

Golf can nicely fit into an affair, perhaps a diversion for the bridal party or down time during a corporate retreat. The course has been acclaimed by *Travel and Leisure Golf Magazine* as one of the 30 best new courses in the world. Renault Winery Resort & Golf is located at 72 N. Bremen Avenue in Egg Harbor City. Joseph's Restaurant is open 7 days a week and serves lunch and dinner. The Renault Winery is open 7 days a week for historic winery tours and tasting. For additional information call (609) 965-2111 or visit the website www.renaultwinery.com.

Famed fountain room (above right). Some of the rare glasses in the Antique Glass Museum (right).

Sheraton Meadowlands
Hotel and Conference Center

The Sheraton Meadowlands Hotel & Conference Center offers one of the region's most versatile conference and banquet venues. Featuring over 30,000 square feet of meeting space, including two magnificent ballrooms which can accommodate up to 1,300 people, it is an ideal place to host a meeting, convention, or social event. The conference center, approved by the International Association of Conference Centers (IACC), consists of 4,100 square feet of meeting space.

Enjoy first-class service and amenities. The Sheraton's catering staff can professionally orchestrate any event from simple ceremonies to lavish receptions. An outstanding combination of warmth and elegance of this lavish hotel combined with all the updated amenities from the just completed $19 million dollar renovation will win the hearts of you and your guests.

To set the stage for your spectacular event, your guests will enter thru a multi-level lobby with plush seating, dramatic lighting, and retro-style murals. A highly skilled culinary team will offer their assistance in tailoring a perfect menu

Executive Boardroom, above, and opposite, lobby.

for your occasion. Whether you are hosting a cocktail party for 100 or banquet for 1000, the Sheraton will guarantee privacy and personalized attention on your wedding day.

Your wedding party and guests can enjoy luxury overnight accommodations featuring Sweet Sleeper beds, The Chairman's Grill and The Lounge for dining and entertainment, an exercise room, indoor pool, and a great cup of coffee from Starbucks, which also provides Internet connections. Many of the comfortable guest rooms feature spectacular views of the New York City skyline.

The Chairman's Grill features traditional American cuisine with a creative twist. Set in an elegant but comfortable atmosphere, diners can

enjoy the freshest ingredients accompanied by impeccable service. Its private dining room is ideal for intimate gatherings or small meetings.

Derby Ballroom setup for a conference.

The just completed $19 million dollar renovation will win the hearts of you and your guests.

The Lounge is a great spot to meet for a drink or light meal after a hard day's work. Located on the lobby level, it combines the charm of a neighborhood tavern with the sparkle and energy of a casual New York City cocktail lounge. A food menu is available during lunch and dinner hours.

Come celebrate in the Sheraton's all-new ballroom and make your day a treasured memory. Your custom package will include extra special arrangements. You will receive a complimentary suite for the bride and groom, complimentary deluxe guestrooms for each set of parents, elegant white glove service, private bridal reception room, choice of solid color floor length tablecloths and matching napkins, directional cards, special guest room rates for out of town guests, and Starwood Preferred Guest Points.

Wedding packages include a festive cocktail reception with a choice of ten butler style hors d'oeuvres and canapés, choice of two action stations, and choice of two cold buffet displays. Dinner proceeds with a Champagne toast, appetizer, salad, and intermezzo.

Entrées include a choice of two gourmet selections served tableside. Possibilities include medallions of veal, morels and chives; breast of chicken stuffed with roasted peppers and mozzarella on a Chianti sauce; grilled swordfish with citrus relish; and duet of filet mignon and jumbo shrimp in a scampi sauce. Desserts will follow and be paired with an elegant tiered wedding cake and coffee service. Throughout the reception enjoy a five-hour premium brand open house bar menu. Of course, the Sheraton's culinary team is available to customize any aspect of this example to meet your individual tastes and desires.

The newly renovated Sheraton Meadowlands Hotel & Conference Center is located at 2 Meadowlands Plaza in East Rutherford, just eight miles from midtown Manhattan. New York City is just across the river and they are only 15 minutes from Newark Liberty Airport. For more information call (201) 896-0500 or visit the website www.sheraton.com/meadowlands.

Opposite, top, a guest room—some feature spectacular views of the New York City skyline. At left, Diamond Ballroom, and above, The Chairman's Grill.

The outside Garden Patio is often the scene for elegant weddings.

Vibrant murals throughout the Stockton Inn, depicting historic scenes or events from the surrounding region, were painted by local artists during the depression in exchange for room & board for their families.

Stockton Inn

Consider the nearly 300 year old Stockton Inn, nestled in the quaint town of Stockton, for your next celebration. Whether it be a wedding, engagement party, anniversary, sweet sixteen, Bar Mitzvahs, or any other special event, the Stockton Inn's rich history envelopes you and your guests right from the onset adding a special charm and character to your celebration.

If you decide to have a grand affair in the garden, where a waterfall flows into a once trout-stocked pond, take comfort in the fact Richard Rodgers and Lorenz Hart were so inspired by this scenic oasis they wrote the now legendary song, "There's a Small Hotel with a Wishing Well." The song was performed in two highly praised Broadway hit musicals, "On Your Toes," in 1936 and "Pal Joey" in 1940.

The outside Garden Patio is often the scene for elegant weddings. There is seating for over 120 guests and the waterfall backdrop can provide a beautiful scene for an outdoor ceremony. The view can also be admired from the inside in the Glass Dining Room. It is a beautiful room overlooking the gardens complete with a baby grande and perfect for any occasion. The room has a very unique and historic silver dollar floor.

The Fox Room, built in early 1900s, is an elegant room perfectly appointed for functions such as holiday parties, business meetings, and special private occasions. Wireless connectivity, and a data LCD projector and screen are modern amenities available. The room still maintains a warm and comfortable historic setting with its large fireplace, wide plank floors, grand windows, and private bar.

You will certainly notice vibrant murals throughout the Stockton Inn. The murals in the original dining rooms were painted primarily by local artists Robert A.D. Miller, begun in 1929 and finished by 1935. Each of the murals depicts an historic scene or event from the surrounding region.

Of course you will want to create your own history while at the inn. With the help of Stockton Inn's dedicated staff, it will be easy to do. Their chef can design an extensive menu for either sit down or buffet style dining. If you would like, the staff can handle every detail, including floral arrangements from their award winning florist, music, and linens. Sandy McGinnis is the catering manager and has years of experience designing elegant affairs.

The Stockton Inn has been prized and cherished by many over the years, even the inn's current owner, Fred Strackhouse, was a fan first. He dined at the inn on numerous occasions and has fond memories celebrating New Year's Eve 1983

This is street side view of the Stockton Inn.

99

There are 11 beautiful bedrooms, suites, and studios (most with fireplaces), perfect for the wedding party's overnight stay, corporate retreat, or weekend getaway.

One of the fireplace suites at the Stockton Inn.

at the inn. It was a desire to continue making history with renewed glory that made this more than twenty-year veteran of the food business take the reigns.

In addition to catering elaborate affairs, the historic Stockton Inn has an elegant restaurant, a rustic tavern, and cozy overnight rooms with many historic touches. Fine dining is served in the exquisite mural rooms with fireside seating during the colder months, and expands to the glass room as spring and summer approaches. In the warmest months of the year, savor your meal and your surroundings and dine alongside the waterfall on their beautiful outside patio.

The Tavern or "Farmer's Bar" has an original molded tin ceiling, and fine mahogany wood detail throughout.

The Stockton Inn's newly renovated guest rooms offer a selection of 11 beautiful bedrooms, suites, and studios (most with fireplaces), perfect for the wedding party's overnight stay, corporate retreat, or weekend getaway.

The Stockton Inn's exquisite facilities are located at 1 Main Street in Stockton. The phone number is (609) 397-1250 and additional information is available on the website at www.stocktoninn.com.

The Stockton Inn's canopied main entrance.

Chapter 3

Grand
Experience

Grand Marquis' famous sought after "Dome Room" with twinkling lights creates a fairytale setting for the most romantic wedding receptions. It's been said that dancing under the dome is like dancing under the stars.

Grand Marquis

◆ ◆ ◆ ◆ ◆ ◆ ◆

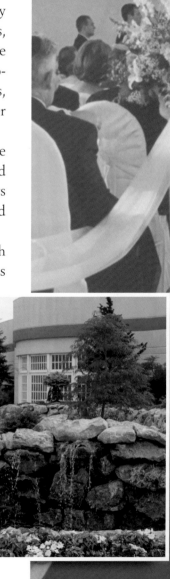

The Grand Marquis, established in 1986, is an exquisite catering facility. The famous sought after "Dome Room" with twinkling lights (pictured on preceding page) creates a fairytale setting for the most romantic wedding receptions, social celebrations, and corporate events. It's been said that dancing under the dome is like dancing under the stars.

Valet parking attendants greet guests who enter a main lobby impeccably accented with baby grand piano, glowing fireplace, sparkling granite floors, and glistening crystal chandelier. The Grand Marquis has a picturesque waterfall garden and is well-equipped for intimate parties of 75, to elaborate grand affairs with seating up to 650. There are private bridal suites, large dance floors, and permanent bars in every room. A separate Kosher kitchen is under Rabbinical supervision 365 days a year.

The Grand Marquis is family owned and operated (and has been since inception in 1986). A member of the family is always present and assisted by a professional staff of highly experienced managers, some with 20 years tenure. The level of personal attention given to each affair is unmatched across the industry.

Executive Chef Adam Livow is a culinary graduate from The French Culinary Institute in New York. Adam is a talented and creative chef. His signature dish is a bone-in filet mignon. He also thrills guests with rack of lamb, chateaubriand, potato crusted sea bass, and veal chops.

Chef Livow supervises a large kitchen staff, including two pastry chefs and an in-house sushi chef. This culinary team can customize menus to any taste or ethnicity and are proficient in Asian, Latin, Russian, Jewish, Greek, and Polish

At right—Ceremony in progress at the Grand Marquis. Inset right is the waterfall garden. Inset far right, a table set in preparation of guests' arrival.

A harpist plays center stage below the dome and surrounded by a lush colorful food display.

as well as other cuisines. The staff will gladly incorporate cherished family recipes into the menu, and baking is done on premise, including elaborate wedding cakes. Brides often bring in a picture of their desired wedding cake for the talented pastry chefs to recreate. Ice sculptures are also crafted in house. Kids receive special treats at the Grand Marquis, such as separate menus, cheese fountains for fries, chocolate fountains, cotton candy, waffle cones, snow cone machines, and sundae bars.

A Grand Marquis wedding cake (left) intricately adorned with numerous edible roses.

106

The Grand Marquis' Viennese table is called a dessert extravaganza and includes everything from a waffle station and crepe station to Italian pastries, apple crisps, fresh fruits, cakes of many varieties, Italian ice cream, sundae bars, and much more.

Both social and corporate events receive the royal treatment. Many corporations and organizations, including IBM, Cisco Systems, PSE&G, L'Oreal, and the New Jersey State Bar Association to name a few, have chosen the Grand Marquis for an exquisitely catered affair as well as for the many amenities available, such as corporate meeting space, audio visual built-in screens and sound systems, and theatre style meetings. The Grand Marquis is located at 1550 Route 9 South in Old Bridge. Call (732) 679-5700 to arrange a personal tour or visit the website www.grandmarquiscaterers.com.

Chef Ferlauto's chateaubriand.

Grand Chalet

When it comes to making your day extra special, Grand Chalet is a perfect place. As a family operated facility, utmost attention and total dedication to every detail is always provided. Great pride is taken in the quality and presentation of the food served. You will be delighted by the elaborate array of continental and ethnic food selections. All of your menu desires can be met by a team of award-winning chefs and culinary experts.

A "Platinum" event is the *"pièce de resistance,"* a sultan's feast extravagant beyond belief. As guests arrive butlers greet them at the door with champagne and strawberries. It proceeds with a fantasy cocktail hour. Lobster, oysters, and other exotic delicacies are everywhere as are white gloved servers purveying the likes of baby racks of lamb, stuffed crab, and more. Grill, pasta, carving, and seafood stations enticingly present even more mouth-watering fare. There still is a full multi-course dinner and "The Grand Finale" Viennese table with a multitude of decadent desserts, including flaming crepes, chocolate fondue fountain, and an international coffee station with choice of cordials.

Personal attention and guidance, which are needed to make any wedding or special occasion truly unique, are supplied through the relationship built with each customer.

At Grand Chalet, newly renovated rooms and top notch service offer an atmosphere of subtle elegance creating the settings for celebrations of any size. Complimentary shuttle service and discounted hotel rates are available for any event booked at Grand Chalet.

Holidays also bring people to Grand Chalet for memorable occasions. Enjoy a candlelit dinner and dancing on Valentine's Day along with special heart shaped desserts for two. Easter features a bunny visit and festive dyed eggs. Mother's Day, Father's Day, and Christmas are always popular and on Thanksgiving–every table receives a turkey. Many other special events are held throughout the year including big band dinner dances and New Year's Day brunch with a complimentary champagne toast.

Grand Chalet is conveniently located on Route 23 in Wayne, New Jersey, and just minutes from Route 46, Route 202, and Interstate 80 and 287. For more information call (973) 633-5111 or visit the website www.grandchalet.com.

The Grand Ballroom bordered by several images of a "Platinum" event in progress.

La Bove Grande

La Bove Grande, a dramatic image appearing as you enter the Lakehurst circle, is the area's preeminent location for celebrating important milestones. A renowned reputation has kept La Bove Grand in demand for both social and corporate affairs. As a major renovation and addition has recently been completed, La Bove Grande sets a new standard for grandeur.

This family owned and operated banquet facility was established in 1974 by Jerry Bove, a 32-year veteran of the food business. He is assisted by family and a dedicated service staff, many with 10 years or more tenure.

The La Bove Grande has much to offer the bride, corporate planner, or any group looking to celebrate in grand style. Weddings, communions, christenings, bar/bat mitzvahs, and corporate events are all hosted with La Bove Grande's signature white glove service. A romantic evening

Main ballroom. Photos ©2006 – RW Hansen/Banquet Services International

awaits you.

A fountain inspired by the fountain of Trevi welcomes guests to La Bove Grande. Enter through a glass enclosed wine cellar display and the admiration for fine cuisine is apparent.

The facility has many architectural details to

Inspired by the fountain of Trevi, La Bove Grande's fountain (opposite) is stunning. Glimpse of gazebo and arched bridge stretching across a small pond (above). On preceding page, La Bove Grande front exterior at dusk. Photos ©2006 – RW Hansen/Banquet Services International.

113

be admired, including elegant granite and marble inlays, cherry wood, and custom carpeting. A beautiful carved cherry wood bar dominates the cocktail room and adjacent is a large outdoor balcony.

The Ballroom accommodates up to two-hundred and fifty guests. It is plush with almond colored carpeting and has Tuscan columns, chandeliers, ornate sconces, and a marble dance floor. The lavish bridal suite has a private balcony overlooking the fountain that is highlighted with lights in the evenings.

Ceremonies can be held in the beautiful outdoor garden area, which includes a pond, waterfall, and gazebo. There is also the Tuscany garden patio offering shade and a cool breeze. La Bove Grand only does one wedding at a time, so the whole place is yours. From the balcony and cocktail room to the manicured grounds, it is one-hundred percent private.

A creative kitchen staff has Vincenzo Bove at the helm and takes pride in everything being freshly prepared in-house. All food is made from scratch with the freshest ingredients. All baking is done on premise. Even the fresh mozzarella cheese is made in-house. The staff is qualified to do elaborate wedding cakes. They can do any ice carving, from bride and groom to hearts with names to a Cinderella theme. They can feature icy corporate logos or names and year for the special anniversary couple.

Other festive culinary presentations include butler hors d'oeuvres and carving stations of top round, racks of lamb, and prime rib au jus. Raw bars, shrimp cocktail bars, and sushi bars are dramatically presented with ice carvings.

Banquets offer options of traditional dishes as well as gourmet entrees such as steak Diane, chateaubriand, Chilean sea bass, trout, Mahi Mahi, chicken Pandora–breast topped with roasted peppers, prosiutto di Parma, and homemade mozzarella with a pimento demi-glaze served over a bed of spinach; veal chops, and chicken Sophia stuffed with sliced fresh orange and Swiss cheese and sautéed in a Grand Marnier sauce.

Within La Bove Grande is a full service fine dining restaurant and lounge called the Circle Landmark. It has a distinguished reputation for Continental cuisine and a lovely dining room with fine linen draped tables, comfortable contoured chairs, and roaring fireplace. A substantial menu features certified Black Angus beef, super fresh seafood, milk fed veal, and is complemented with a comprehensive wine list.

La Bove Grande is located in Lakehurst at 800 State Highway 70. Dinner and lunch is served seven days a week in the Circle Landmark Restaurant. Lavish yearly events include New Year's Eve gala, Easter celebration, Mother's Day, and Thanksgiving.

For additional information on banquets or a la cart dining call (732) 657-8377 or visit www.circleland mark.com/home.

Clockwise (from opposite top left) Private dining room. Carved cherry wood bar. Foyer furnished with finely crafted temperature controlled wine cabinets. Photos ©2006 – RW Hansen/Banquet Services International

Stately front entrance of Macaluso's.

Macaluso's

Experience the majesty that is... Macaluso's. A breathtaking facility with Mediterranean charm, Macaluso's has a grand ballroom with newly

(From the left) Bride and groom rest on a neoclassical garden bench. Fresh fruit display with ice sculpture. Bride and groom by waterfall.

appointed details and magnificent courtyards. Incredibly attentive service, unique presentations, and legendary cuisine give rise to a truly memorable affair. Cocktail Hour and Venetian table are flamboyant specialties.

Your special day begins in the "Cocktail Lounge" where distinctive cuisine will tempt and satisfy even the most discerning palette. World class professionals stand ready to serve you like royalty. Unique presentations and customized ice sculptures will take your breath away.

Once the Cocktail Hour is completed, the doors will open into the "Grand Ballroom." The bride and groom will make their first appearance as a married couple, as they descend the elegant curved staircase into the ballroom. Awaiting them are their honored guests and a fabulous five-course culinary experience.

The evening climaxes as the happy couple is escorted to the "Venetian Room" where a confectionery concerto of taste tempting sweets await their approval. As they welcome their guests to join

them for delicious French and Italian pastries, coffees and cordials, the evening seems to never end.

Your "special day" truly deserves a "special place." From the very beginning of your affair, to the final toast, every detail will be carefully attended to ensure that you and your guests will long remember the majesty that is… Macaluso's.

Macaluso's is owned and operated by the Mattar family and located at 161 Rea Avenue in Hawthorne. For more information call (973) 427-7320 or visit the website www.macalusos.com.

Food art ala Macaluso's (above right). Ballroom featuring grand entrance staircase.

A Collection of Insightful Comments from Past Brides and Grooms

Distinguished logo of Macaluso's.

"Our wedding (was held) almost 4 months ago and we still receive so many compliments on how unbelievable and how wonderful Macaluso's was. You truly made our wedding a magical, memorable fairy tale come true!"
–Gineen & Bill S.

"You and your staff were unbelievable in every way! From the planning, all the time you spent with us, and all the phone calls, to the actual day – everything was beyond perfect! We couldn't have asked for more. People are still raving!"
–Kristen & Karim H.

"Thank you very much for making our special day such a memorable one, not only for us, but for all of our guests. We would highly recommend Macaluso's for any occasion. The two of us felt like royalty and were able to enjoy ourselves that night!"
–Gina & Leo C.

Juliet balcony (above) and cold shellfish display (opposite) presented in an elaborate custom crafted seafood boat.

"The food, help and atmosphere was outstanding. From the start of the evening to the finish, every detail of our wedding seemed to be thought out with no chance for there to be a mistake. Some of our favorite pictures were taken in front of the small waterfall. Once again, we're very thankful for your help in making our wedding one that we and our guests will be talking about for years!"
–Chris & Sarah M.

"We don't even know where to begin. Our wedding far exceeded our expectations and we know we have all of you to thank. The service, the ambiance, and the food were just superb and elegant. Our guests continue to say it was the best wedding they've ever attended."
–Michael & Kerri Anne T.

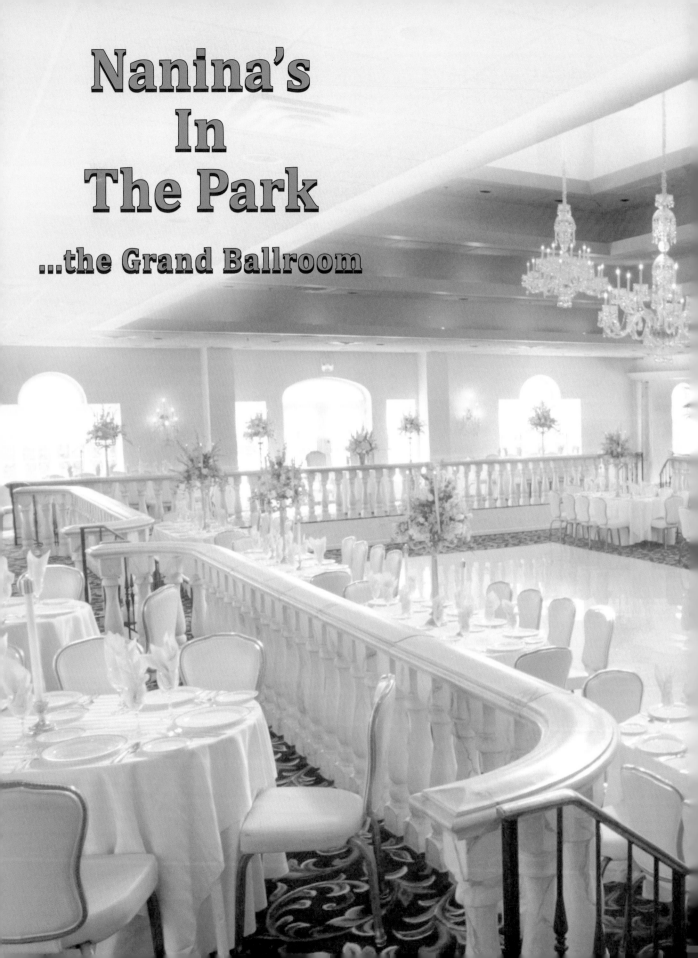

Nanina's In The Park

...the Grand Ballroom

Charming front entrance of Nanina's In The Park.

Ceremony taking place under the Florentine arbor.

anina's In The Park is a magnificent New Jersey landmark, nestled in a historical park setting. Nanina's presents you with more than 50 years of catering tradition and a spectacular multimillion-dollar renovation. The lavishly manicured grounds, complete with garden terrace waterfalls, stream with your personal bridge, and Florentine arbor, provide the perfect backdrop for your outdoor ceremony and cocktail hour. Winding marble staircases, a "Juliet" balcony, and hand-painted cathedral ceilings are just a few of the amenities that embody this Tuscan villa architecture. The

The library trimmed in mahogany and featuring a vintage neoclassic fireplace.

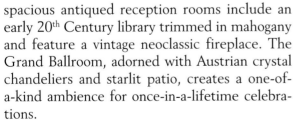

spacious antiqued reception rooms include an early 20th Century library trimmed in mahogany and feature a vintage neoclassic fireplace. The Grand Ballroom, adorned with Austrian crystal chandeliers and starlit patio, creates a one-of-a-kind ambience for once-in-a-lifetime celebrations.

A family owned and operated venue famed for original Italian cuisine, Nanina's reputation for excellence has continued for generations. Nanina's In The Park has an unrivaled reputation for its incomparable menu. Every affair starts with their premium package and includes Nanina's best

of the best, which includes Nanina's best of the best seafood bars and ends with their Viennese displays.

Master Chef Vincenzo, who has been with Nanina's since its inception, is famous in his own rite for his authentic recipes. After thousands of rave reviews regarding Chef Vincenzo's original pasta sauces and Italian delicacies, Nanina's has answered the public's request for access to their products. In December of 2005, Nanina's In The Park Gourmet Sauce made its debut at Monmouth University to 380 guests from area businesses, and met with unprecedented success. The school's entrepreneurial class chose Nanina's In the Park and Chef Vincenzo for their class project that year. Building on their original venture, Nanina's has designed, developed and brought forth to the general public (with discerning palates...) a line of delectable, homemade, gourmet Italian sauces. Now available at your local grocer or via the web are Nanina's original Marinara, Vodka Sauce, Fra Diavolo, and Tomato Basil. Recognizing the hard work and effort put forth by both the students and the university, Nanina's has earmarked a portion of the profits for an entrepreneurial scholarship for the students of Monmouth University in appreciation of their efforts.

If exceptional cuisine, impeccable service, and unsurpassed presentation are not enough, their unique location will positively captivate you.

123

Versatile use of Nanina's gourmet Italian sauces (above) includes draping over fresh seafood. Master Chef Vincenzo (below) has been with Nanina's since its inception. And opposite, Nanina's original Marinara Sauce and Vodka Sauce are now available at your local grocer or via the web.

Located on the cusp of New Jersey's renowned Branch Brook Park, Nanina's exquisite property is surrounded by thousands of flowering Cherry Blossom trees in season, creating a picture perfect setting you must see to believe. All of this truly establishes Nanina's In The Park as a stunning landmark.

Convenient to all major highways and just three minutes from the Garden State Parkway, Nanina's has resided in the same location for more than 50 years. Nanina's offers the ideal venue for remarkable catered events, including spectacular weddings, distinguished corporate affairs, and all your family celebrations. Their Ballroom is reserved exclusively for one affair at a time and spaciously accommodates up to 400 seated guests.

Visit their facility and see the splendor for yourself. Contact them for a guided tour at 973-751-1230. Via the website www.naninasinthepark.com, you can preview their venue and obtain more information about their gourmet products. Nanina's In The Park is located at 540 Mill Street in Belleville.

Bride and groom (left) descend the curved staircase making their grand entrance into the Beau Palais Room. (Below) Images of a party—flowers, hors d'oeuvres, and the irresistible chocolate fountain.

Paris Caterers
at
The Palace

One of New Jersey's newest catering facilities, Paris Caterers at The Palace, offers first-rate cuisine, professional service, and a classy atmosphere to turn any special occasion into a spectacular affair. Their professional staff will assist you in every way to make sure your event will go smoothly. Whether you are planning a wedding, Bar Mitzvah, Bat Mitzvah, corporate function, office party, or any other social event, Paris Caterers' attention to detail will ensure you have an event to remember.

Paris Caterers has been in business since 1993 and their new facility was designed to accommodate the newest trends for celebrating in style. From a state-of-the-art sound system to sophisticated décor, your guests will be impressed.

Owners/brothers Keith and Robert Eshelman create a dynamic team and contribute their own expertise to Paris Caterers. Keith, owning one of the area's top entertainment companies focusing on DJing and emceeing, incorporates a phenomenal audiovisual experience into affairs at Paris Caterers. Enjoy a dance floor that "rocks," while at the same time volume levels tableside allow conversation to continue. Don't underestimate the power of great audiovisuals to enhance your celebration. A built-in 7 by 10 foot video screen not only gives all your guests a perfect seat, it has brought guests to tears of joy. A bride's dance with her father has never been more emotional than when simulcast with live coverage alternating with photos from childhood.

Master Chef Robert Eshelman, a graduate of the Culinary School at Atlantic County Community College, amassed several prestigious credentials. He's apprenticed at the Ritz Carlton, Philadelphia and worked at the legendary Hideaway for 13 years. His contribution at

Paris Caterers is gastronomic pleasures. Chef Robert is adept in Cajun cuisine, specializes in French sauces and his menu, personally customized for clients, can feature anything from medallions of filet mignon with a wild mushroom sauce and topped with crabmeat to chicken cordon blue.

Paris Caterers at The Palace has three banquet rooms and features a two-story foyer with a stately Y-staircase. The Magnificent Beau Palais room has a beauti-

ful curved staircase leading to the dance floor for that grand entrance of the bride and groom, and seating for up to 450 guests. The Garden Room also has a staircase, seating for up to 350 guests, and access to a lovely garden where you can have your wedding ceremony or capture some wonderful photos. Both rooms have a gas fireplace for ambience, plus tastefully appointed bridal suites for the bride, groom, and bridal party. The third room, called the Paris Room, is more

intimate, has its own private entrance, and seating for up to 250 guests.

Every Wednesday is vendor day and clients are welcome to come on premise and talk to all types of professionals who can assist in your party plans. They include everything from photographers, limousine services, DJ's, makeup and hair stylists, videographers, florists, travel agents, and formalwear merchants.

The Paris Caterers at The Palace are located at 109 N. Black Horse Pike in Blackwood.

The phone number is (856) 374-2000 and more information can be found on the website www.paris-caterers.com.

(Above from the left) Banquet Manager, Frank Bigwood is an eight year veteran of the catering business. Owner/Master Chef Robert Eshelman. Owner/Marketing & Sales Director Keith Eshelman. (Left and from bottom left) Two views of the distinguished front entrance, hors d'oeuvres, and a wedding cake. (Bottom right) The bride and flower girl, comfortable in the bridal suite, peer out into the ballroom.

Pictured is a rendition of The
Westin Mt. Laurel and the luxury
to follow its opening—fine cuisine,
the art of a pastry chef, and
exquisite table settings.

The Westin
Mt. Laurel

The new Westin Mt. Laurel will attempt to redefine luxury in South Jersey. The management team desires to make this world-class hotel become a destination for business and leisure travelers, and become part of the fabric of the South Jersey social community. The hotel will open in the fall of 2007.

Upon entering the Westin Mt. Laurel, one will marvel at the shimmering glass curtain wall and the use of rich dark woods accented by limestone and marble architectural design elements. The new Westin Mt. Laurel will be a venue for celebrating special occasions.

The hotel's manicured gardens and sweeping views will create the perfect setting for a romantic or corporate event. The Westin will feature approximately 200 guestrooms, 20,000 square feet of ballrooms and meeting space, a contemporary restaurant with lounge and a private wine cellar for intimate dining for 15-30 guests. There will also be a Coffee Bar and an indoor pool.

For those planning a wedding or special event, the Westin Mt. Laurel is ideally situated off all major highways and is just minutes from downtown Philadelphia.

The graceful 6,000 square foot Grand Ballroom is being built to exude luxury while allowing maximum flexibility for a gala ball or even an intimate dinner. Both ballrooms are designed to accommodate receptions of up to 500 guests. The European-style elegance will impress both social and corporate guests alike; and include the custom pattern carpet, picture windows as well as the Austrian crystal chandeliers that will adorn the halls.

Guests will dine on Royal Doulton English china and indulge in the cuisine of award winning, internationally trained, Chef Mirko Loeffler, CCC, CEC, whose training includes stints at some of the most exclusive restaurants and hotels in the world.

"The Westin Mt. Laurel will offer all the elements of elegance, expected in a world-class hotel," said Eric Davies, Regional General Manager of The Wurzak Hotel Group, "With the Westin brand our hotel will raise the bar to the highest level for everyone in Southern New Jersey."

All guestrooms at the Westin Mt. Laurel will feature Westin's signature Heavenly Bed®, internet access, flat-panel televisions, cordless phone, executive work desk, and Westin's Heavenly Bath®. Many guest rooms will also feature floor-to-ceiling glass windows with expansive views.

The Heavenly Bath® is an industry first, offering guests a luxurious shower, with a dual showerhead and a revolutionary curved shower rod, allowing for a much more relaxed, less confined experience. The Heavenly Bath® also features Brazilian combed cotton bath sheets and custom-designed velour bathrobes. Additionally, many baths at the Westin Mt. Laurel will include separate glass-enclosed stone showers and deep soaking tubs.

Powered by Reebok Gym, is the Westin Mt. Laurel's complimentary fitness facility. The gym will include treadmills, elliptical trainers, step machines, and bikes that all face personal, flat-screen televisions. The gym will offer a variety of body-toning weight machines and free weights, as well as towels and headphones.

The entire property like all Westin hotels is part of the Breath Westin Program. The smoke-free hotel allows all guests a comfortable, healthy environment. Research has shown that 92% of all Westin hotel guests preferred a smoke-free room, precipitating Westin to establish this policy and become the first smoke-free, upscale, hotel brand in America.

The Westin Mt. Laurel is located at 555 Fellowship Road in Mt. Laurel. For more information please call (856) 778-7300 or visit the website www.westinmtlaurel.com.

Chapter 4

Mirror images of a tablesetting at The Gables.

Intimate Celebrations

The Gables

The beach has always been a lure for romantic weddings and spirited celebrations. The Gables, located in Beach Haven, adds the charm of a Victorian inn. A total renovation, begun in 2005, revitalized this remarkable landmark and preserved its period detail. It remains a vital part of historic Beach Haven, offering a warm welcome, glorious food, and gracious lodging.

Built by the Cahill family in 1892 and then called Kathlyn Cottage, the roomy front porch led to the foyer, parlor, and a large dining room, just as it still does today. Upstairs, a warren of 14 small bedrooms housed Beach Haven's life-guards, and a sleeping porch provided respite on hot summer nights. Centrally located, the house served over the years as a postal drop, an all girls' boarding house, a produce market, and the venue for the first annual Beach Haven Fire Department Chicken Dinner. Purchased in the 1970s by Lucy Reddington, Green Gables, as it was then called, was turned into the island's first bed and breakfast. A decade later, Lucy sold her business to a dynamic Italian couple, Adolfo DiMartino and Rita Rapella, who obtained planning permission to open a restaurant at the inn. They added a professional kitchen, enlarged the dining room–and earned four stars from the *New York Times* food critics. In 2005, Sondra and Steve Beninati bought the century-old Folk Victorian house on Long Beach Island. Sondra Beninati had a dream. She wanted to restore this community gathering spot to its former glory, and run it as an inn. Together, the Beninatis watched the venerable old house undergo extensive structural repairs. In addition to the state-of-the-art professional kitchen, it now boasts air conditioning and the addition of 10 fireplaces, not to mention a new roof. The warren of upstairs rooms has given way to five luxurious guest bedrooms with period furnishings and marble bathrooms. The backyard Victorian garden, Kathlyn Court, with its columned pergola, brick patio, and stone fountain, is now available for dining al fresco, weddings, and private events. Sondra Beninati brings more than an unerring aesthetic instinct to running The Gables; she has a strong background in the hospitality business. She worked at Tavern on the Green in Central Park in New York; at Holloran House Hotel, and at Spadeus in Italy. No stranger to the food industry, Steve Beninati

Bailey Lloyd Room (above left), Chapel Room (above right) and (opposite) Victoria Albert Room.

Pasta being rolled out by hand. The tradition of fine cuisine continues at The Gables.

acts as a consultant for The Gables Inn and Restaurant. He co-founded Everything Yogurt, the originator of the frozen yogurt shop and Colombo Yogurt's first retailer, which in its heyday had over 300 stores nationwide.

This beautifully restored inn provides just the right setting for an intimate wedding and reception. In summer and fall, you can opt for the flower-filled garden courtyard (the bride can make a fabulous entrance through the vine-covered pergola); in winter, a crackling log fire in the large parlor and gracious dining room and a sweeping staircase add magical touches. The entire inn can accommodate over 100 for a sit-down reception. The parlor and two other lovely dining rooms can be used individually for smaller private parties.

Flowers, musical entertainment, audio speaker, and tents are available by special arrangement. Catering is also available. The Gables is located at 212 Centre Street in Beach Haven. For more details, please call 1-(888) LBI-Gables or visit The Gables website at www.gableslbi.com.

(Below, from the left) Front exterior, service to the backyard garden, Kathlyn Court; stacked presentation of fresh mozzarella and heirloom tomatoes and Kathlyn Court.

Buddakan

✦ ✦ ✦ ✦ ✦ ✦ ✦

Buddakan is a thrill–"dining theater"–where energetic, well trained servers, exotic food and drink, and a fantasy interior meld compatibly together setting the stage for a festive party. Following the tradition of Asian cultures, Buddakan provides a family style dining experience by offering plentiful portions designed to be shared. Enjoy King Crab Tempura with a sweet & sour ponzu sauce, Kobe Beef Satays, and Wasabi Crusted Filet Mignon. Specialty cocktails include the Bonsai-made with Grey Goose Vodka and fresh cilantro and a sake list offers Kaika Kaze No Ichirin–refreshing, floral, and sweet with a silky finish aka "Flower in Wind."

Enter Stephen Starr's temple of modern Asian cuisine and proceed through an enchanted Asian garden surrounded by multi-colored archways, 25-foot tall trees that appear to grow through the ceiling, rocks and foot bridges, to arrive at the awe inspiring restaurant's main dining room. A twilight sky illuminated with state-of-the-art lighting, reclaimed Douglas fir wood covered walls, and a façade of houses with clay tile roofs create the illusion of being inside the courtyard of an ancient Chinese village. A series of "opium den" style rooms provide guests with semi-private dining nooks while a gigantic golden Buddha watches over the entire restaurant from the head of a 24-foot long onyx communal dining table that accommodates 22 guests.

Buddakan can host intimate gatherings or large receptions in several areas of the restaurant. The main rooms are located on the left and right sides of the communal table. Each area seats up to sixty guests for seated dinner. Overlooking the main dining room, the mezzanine features a private bar and accommodates up to forty-eight guests for seated dinners or sixty-five guests for a standing reception. The entire restaurant is also available for events where you and your guests will enjoy Buddakan exclusively. The restaurant is able to seat two-hundred guests for dinner and up to three-hundred guests for a standing reception.

Buddakan is located at One Atlantic Ocean in The Pier Shops at Caesars in Atlantic City. The $200 million Pier features a 400-foot wrap-around boardwalk atop a fabricated beach-scape, with dunes, grass, and windows that provide panoramic views of the actual beach and ocean outside. The magnificent promenade leads to the restaurants' entrances. Buddakan is a 9,000-square-foot venue. For special events call (609) 674-0100. Additional information can be found on the website www.buddakanac.com.

Buddakan's onyx communal dining table has seating for twenty-two and overlooks a gigantic golden Buddha.

Fiorino's global wine collection received the coveted Award of Excellence from Wine Spectator Magazine.

Fiorino photographs courtesy of Verdini Studios.

Fiorino

Mentor Bitici adds a final touch.

Pan-seared Branzino with julianne of vegetables, roasted fennel mashed potatoes. Fine wine and Italian cheese—Fiorino specialties (below).

Fiorino means gold coin of Florence and this restaurant certainly could be coined a treasure. Once inside you immediately get that old world feeling of Florence. Beautiful paintings of Italian and Roman scenes adorn the walls. Friendly waiters greet you and make you feel right at home. Owner John Bitici and his two sons, Mentor and Ilir, make wonderful hosts and will graciously accommodate your aspirations, whether it is a catered affair, special celebration, or evening of relaxed fine dining.

Fiorino's stunning décor and soothing ambience will enhance any private party experience. They can accommodate up to 60 guests for catered affairs and up to 120 by request. There is a comprehensive wine list, recognized with the Award of Excellence by *Wine Spectator* Magazine. A second list offers all wines at $22 a bottle. There is even an elegant wine room for private parties and ala carte dining on the weekends. The Academy of Hospitality Science awarded Fiorino with the coveted Five Star Diamond Award for outstanding food and service. The Star-Ledger gave Fiorino ☆☆☆½; and about the chef said, "Espinoza has made grilling an art form."

Rack of venison with red wine and gooseberries.

Seafood avacodo.

A chocolate bombe celebration cake.

Chef Carlos Espinoza, a native of El Salvador, led the kitchen for two decades at John's New York City restaurants. John has sent him on numerous occasions to Tuscany to study the local cuisine, which he now incorporates into the food prepared at the restaurant. His unique menu includes marinated grilled octopus with a warm potato salad; grilled quail over wild mushroom risotto and arugula; steamed red snapper with saffron, fennel, mussels, and clams; and grilled veal chop with porcini mushroom orzo and roasted baby greens. There are ten to twelve intriguing specials prepared and printed with the regular menu every day. The menu changes seasonally. During the fall, game such as venison, ostrich, rabbit and pheasant will often be featured. In addition to wonderful food, tables are comfortably spaced, good acoustics allow intimate conversation, and service is superb.

Wine tasting dinners are scheduled throughout the year. The entire restaurant is available for catered affairs on Sundays. Fiorino Ristorante is located at 38 Maple Street in Summit. The phone number is (908) 277-1900. Additional information can be found on the website www.fiorinoristorante.com.

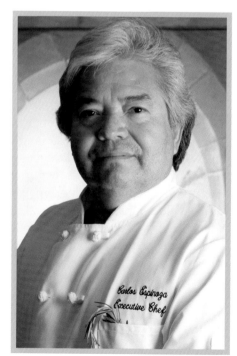

Chef Carlos Espinoza–highly respected for his brilliant culinary skills.

Owners Tricia and David DiCenso.

The Greenhouse

Expect the best when you visit The Greenhouse in Wayne. New owners, Tricia and David DiCenso, totally renovated the upstairs of The Greenhouse in 2003. With the new look they introduced a delicious new menu full of rich Italian recipes featuring an array of pasta, seafood, veal, chicken, pork, and beef dishes. To complement your meal, a well thought out wine list offering wine by the glass and bottle has been created. In addition, there is a full bar headlining classic cocktails.

The Greenhouse is a perfect place for your next party, whether it is a bridal or baby shower, an engagement celebration, rehearsal dinner, or any other social event where you want an atmosphere out of the ordinary. The upstairs party rooms, decorated with warm golden tones and fresh white linens on the tables, are able to entertain up to 95 people comfortably.

For your event you can choose from a selection of party packages that are offered and even print a specially designed menu for your guests to take as a keepsake. Whether you are interested in a buffet or a sit down dinner, your food will be prepared to order with the freshest of foods and the finest of ingredients. It will be brought to you by a staff that is well trained and prides itself on giving you superb service. Your every need will be attended to so you can feel like a guest at your own party.

The Greenhouse is located at 611 Ratzer Road in Wayne, easily accessible from Routes 23, 46, 80, and 287. The restaurant and bar are open seven days a week serving both lunch and dinner and the party rooms are also available seven days. The phone number is (973) 305-1180. Their website is www.greenhousecafenj.com.

A seafood special—Salmon prepared with a light red sauce and a touch of herbs surrounded by clams, mussels, shrimp and scallops.

Upstairs party rooms, decorated with warm golden tones and fresh white linens on the tables, are able entertain up to 95 people comfortably.

Wrought iron gated private room. Photography courtesy of Verdini Studios.

Lahiere's

One of the state's longest running hospitality establishments, Lahiere's is a popular choice for catered affairs and fine dining. On any give night there are usually several groups celebrating anything from a special birthday or anniversary to a corporate function. Because of their many rooms of varying sizes they are ideal for intimate to elegant celebrations.

The cuisine is incredibly flavorful and artistically presented. Sourcing the finest and freshest ingredients and preparing beguiling sauces from time honored techniques has lured a savvy dining crowd to this establishment.

It all began in 1915 when Joseph Christen moved from Zurich, Switzerland, to Manhattan, where he worked as Maitre d' at the Ritz Carlton. That same year Mary Louise Lahiere moved from the South of France to Montreal. In 1916, she also moved to New York where she worked at the Plaza Hotel. Joseph and Mary Louise met, fell in love, and married in 1917.

In 1919, Joseph and Mary Louise moved to Princeton to open a restaurant with Mary Louise's two brothers, Jean Pierre and Eugene. However, less than one year after opening Lahiere's, Mary Louise's two brothers who farmed Lambert's farm on Rosedale Road, went back to farming full time.

In 1927, Leon Joseph Christen was born. He graduated from Princeton University in 1949 with a degree in mechanical engineering and went on to earn his M.B.A. from Columbia University in 1952. He married Rosemarie Simone in 1952 and they moved to Canada in 1956 working for Johnson & Higgins, the insurance company.

In 1961, after the passing of Mary Louise, Leon and Rosemarie moved back to Princeton to manage Lahiere's with Leon's father. They brought their young daughters, Caroline and Michele. Joe Christen was born four years later.

Joe Christen now operates Lahiere's, which he has been doing for the past 12 years. Joe formally started with the restaurant upon his graduation from the University of Colorado at Boulder in 1987. He and his wife, Jill, have two daughters, Simone and Julia.

Today, Lahiere's serves contemporary American cuisine as compared to its strictly French predecessor. The restaurant welcomes its new chef, Paul Robinson, who has been the sous chef at Lahiere's for over 12 years, and is a graduate of the Culinary Institute of America in Hyde Park, New York. The restaurant is also fortunate to have General Manager David Wagner, a 25-year veteran and also a CIA alum, wine and beverage manager Chris Canavari, and Paul's wife Jennifer, Lahiere's pastry chef.

The restaurant may appear modest in size with its many cozy rooms, but can seat up to 200 patrons at once. While you do not see their photographs on the walls, a range of luminaries have enjoyed Lahiere's, including King Hussein of Jordan, James Baker, Paul Newman, Reggie White, Donald Sutherland, and Bob Hope. Princeton's own John Chancellor used to be a regular.

Lahiere's is located at 5-11 Witherspoon Street in Princeton. For further information call (609) 921-2798 or visit the website www.lahieres.com.

One of the upstairs private rooms ideal for rehersal dinners and business meetings.

LouCas

*L*ouCas is both a highly praised restaurant and a first-rate banquet facility. An astonishing number of voracious diners swarm LouCas nightly for cuisine praised by the *New York Times* and *The Star-Ledger*. Both regular diners and corporate clients include Loucas cuisine as part of their most important celebrations, whether it be an intimate party or momentous occassion.

LouCas had a stellar opening in 1991. The collaboration between chefs Loucas Sofocli and Alex Charalambous immediately stirred things up on the New Jersey dining scene. It was flavorful food arising from the highest quality ingredients and very skillful hands in the kitchen that ignited the public's attention. Coupled with a distinguished atmosphere, Loucas had a winning formula. Today it is clear to see time has only made LouCas better. The formula is the same and diligence and perseverance brought continued success. Through expansions and renovations Loucas Sofocli and Alex Charalambous have kept their prestigious position amongst New Jersey's culinary elite.

The atmosphere at LouCas is stunning and has evolved with the times. The Garden room accommodates private parties of up to 120 people or 100 with dance and has murals adorning many of the walls. The Garden Room Alcove can accommodate private parties up to 16 people. Its glass enclosure and French doors offer secluded privacy.

The new dining room has a beautifully adorned cathedral ceiling and can accommodate private parties of up to 50 people. A banquet at LouCas pairs fine cuisine with gracious service. They specialize in business functions, showers, engagements, rehearsal dinners, anniversary, retirements, christenings, bar mitzvahs, and bat mitzvahs.

The menu highlights Italian cuisine, with a special emphasis on seafood. *The Star-Ledger* gave LouCas "☆☆☆½" and said, "A cut above. Impeccably fresh, high-quality ingredients are cooked with respect and restraint, enhanced just so. Dishes are beautifully presented in King Kong-size portions, and reasonably priced to boot."

LouCas is located at 9 Lincoln Highway (Route 27) in Edison. LouCas is available seven days a week for lunch, dinner, and private functions. For more information call (732) 549-8580 or visit the website www.loucasrestaurant.com.

This new dining room (opposite) can accommodate private parties of up to 50 people. The Garden Room Alcove (above left) can accommodate private parties of up to 16 people. The main room (above) will accommodate private parties of up to 150.

Ponte Vecchio

onte Vecchio is the latest collaboration from the LouCas family of restaurants. This Italian seafood grill specializes in serving the finest seafood, along with the best traditional Italian cuisine. The décor of this 180 seat facility is based upon the famous "Ponte Vecchio" bridge in Florence, Italy.

Ponte Vecchio means "Old Bridge" and it is the oldest bridge in Florence crossing the River Arno. So greatly admired, it was built by Neri di Fioravanle in 1345 with three stone arches. It is characterized by the small houses that line both sides of the bridge. Today, the bridge is home to numerous shops and boutiques. During the warmer months Ponte Vecchio is filled with visitors, street performers, and artists.

With three separate dining rooms, Ponte Vecchio's lavish settings are perfect for a private

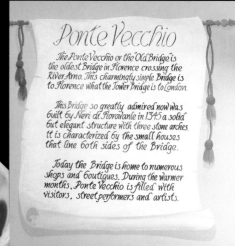

Ponte Vecchio

The Ponte Vecchio or the "Old Bridge" is the oldest Bridge in Florence crossing the River Arno. This charmingly simple Bridge is to Florence what the Tower Bridge is to London.

This Bridge so greatly admired now was built by Neri di Fioravanle in 1345 a solid but elegant structure with three stone arches. It is characterized by the small houses that line both sides of the Bridge.

Today the Bridge is home to numerous shops and boutiques. During the warmer months, Ponte Vecchio is filled with visitors, street performers and artists.

Clockwise from left—This room's décor includes a depiction of the Ponte Vecchio Bridge, wide framed mirror, and wrought iron accents. Ponte Vecchio's Bouillabaisse—a medley of fresh seafood and shellfish simmered in a mild savory sauce with a hint of Pernod and fresh vegetables. Mural of scroll inscribed with "Old Bridge" story vividly denotes Ponte Vecchio's motif. Pan seared halibut over sauteed spinach topped with jumbo lump crabmeat, shiitake mushrooms, artichoke hearts, and sundried tomatoes finished in a chardonnay buerre blanc.

party or for an evening of relaxed and casual fine dining. Celebrate your special occasion in their banquet room which can accommodate up to 100 people. Their corporate dining room can accommodate up to 40 people. Ponte Vecchio specializes in business functions, showers, rehearsal dinners, engagements, anniversaries, retirements, christenings, Bar Mitzvahs, and Bat Mitzvahs.

With their emphasis on seafood you could choose to serve Chilean sea bass, lobster tails, or red snapper at your party. Ponte Vecchio offers many other delicacies from the sea and interesting selections of chicken, lamb, beef, veal, as well as memorable pastas. Special appetizers to get the festivities started can include rock shrimp arabiatta, crab cakes, shrimp cocktail, baby lamb chops, and a cold seafood cocktail.

Ponte Vecchio is located at 3863 Route 516 East in Old Bridge. For more information call (732) 607-1650 or visit the website www.restaurantpontevecchio.com.

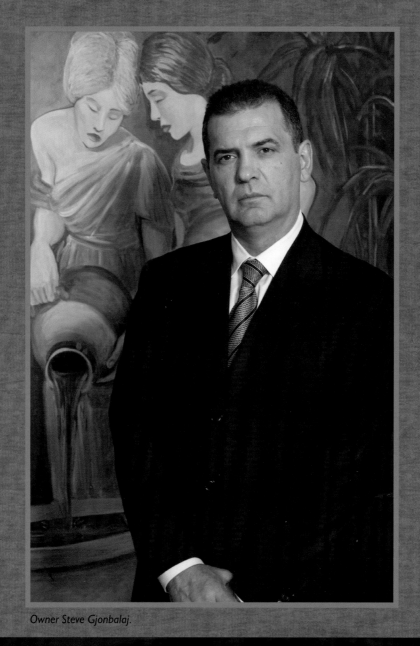

Owner Steve Gjonbalaj.

SamVera

SamVera, a grandiose Northern Italian restaurant located in Central New Jersey horse country, is the brainchild of longtime restaurateur Steve Gjonbalaj, who owned four restaurants in New York City. SettColli, the most renown of the four, received

a four star rating on numerous occasions.

It was a chance encounter, while driving along Route 520 in Marlboro, which set the wheels in motion. Gjonbalaj saw a Victorian home for sale that he envisioned could be transformed into a pristine dining destination. His son Sam

Much of the décor pays homage to fine wines(above). One of several rooms within SamVera (below).

and niece Vera provided the inspiration for the name. A major construction project brought the vision to a reality. With no resemblance to its former structure, SamVera is a posh retreat serving exceptional cuisine and providing impeccable service. A Kathy Rosemilia interior design sets the tone for luxurious Italian experience. There are exquisite antiques and dazzling appointments throughout. A mural, depicting three wine maidens, is the predominant focal point in a plush cocktail lounge. Open air terraces laid with granite flooring accommodate seating for dining al fresco.

Ample parking, manicured grounds, and a Central New Jersey location in combination with an admired culinary reputation have put SamVera's Banquet facilities in high demand. Breathtaking private rooms are perfect for dinner parties, meetings, rehearsal dinners, or small dramatic weddings.

Kitchen and service staffs include long time regulars of Gjonbalaj's employ. Many are loyal

comrades from his previous New York restaurants. Several have been with Gjonbalaj for nearly twenty years. This tenured staff is an invaluable asset in the hospitality business.

The menu reflects intriguing interpretations of Northern Italian cuisine and the chef takes advantage of seasonal foods. Enjoy chilled seafood salad featuring octopus, calamari, scungilli, shrimp, fresh celery, gaeta olives, garlic, lemon juice, and a touch of clam juice; penne ala vodka; and bass marechiare. Rolling carts bring the excitement of tableside service. Specialties include Dover sole de-boned tableside, crepes Suzette, and raspberry or bananas flambé. SamVera has a world-class wine list featuring over 400 bottles.

SamVera is located at 476 Route 520 in Marlboro. They are available for private parties and dinner seven days a week. Lunch is served Monday through Friday. Their phone number is (732)834-9889. Additional information is available on the website www.samvera.com.

Double veranda and meticulous landscaping (left) at SamVera's Southern exposure. Veranda view (above). Fresh flowers—always influencing the SamVera atmosphere (right).

Chapter 5
Pristine Surroundings

The exquisite gardens of The Estate at Florentine Gardens.

Bride and groom's arrival (above). One of several fountains on the grounds (below). Bride and groom (right) pose on winding brick path.

The Estate
at
Florentine Gardens

The Estate at Florentine Gardens is a majestical oasis for social and corporate affairs. Tom Daidone has owned The Estate since 1989 and made extensive renovations in 2000. His five million dollar overhaul has made The Estate into a revered choice for special occasions.

Words alone can't describe the beauty and romance of a wedding at this magnificent Georgian estate. They host only one elegant wedding at a time, so on your special day, the entire estate is yours, including acres of meticulously manicured grounds.

Enjoy the splendor of exquisite gardens with heirloom roses, a private bridal garden for unforgettable photos, and dramatic luminescent fountains. Admire the beauty from unique coves or follow winding brick pathways leading to picturesque stone gazebos. Trees are lit with twinkle lights and create a spectacular view. The pristine gardens are an ideal setting for a romantic outdoor ceremony.

Unsurpassed cuisine is presented in abundance

and with distinctive flair. Enjoy the thrill of an elaborate culinary banquet. Everything from butler served hors d'oeuvres and carving and pasta stations to Brazilian rodizio, dim sum, and a ceviche bar are available to light up the party and gastronomically delight every guest. Cocktail hour takes place in a separate cocktail room with enough seating for everyone to enjoy the array of food. The dinner reception follows and may include duck leg confit, chilled shrimp martini, chateaubriand, or rosemary crusted rack of lamb.

Ideally positioned to view the gardens day or night, the Grand Ballroom is surrounded by floor to ceiling windows and features impressive twenty-two foot high ceilings, a stately mahogany fireplace, breathtaking ten foot crystal chandeliers, and a magnificent Juliet balcony–perfect for tossing the bouquet.

The final crescendo is the Viennese hour–a luxurious offer-

ing of delectable desserts. The Estate's famed "Sweets, Smoke and Jazz" adds an extra hour to your affair and guests enjoy a three piece jazz ensemble, cigar bar, decadent display of cakes, tarts, and butler passed truffles, chocolate, and confections. Keep the party going with a custom 2-hour after party package that includes a full Viennese hour and entertainment.

Exclusivity of the entire facility to your affair allows for an exemplary level of service. All the staffs

Multi-layers of sculpted hedges and vibrant flowers distinguish this brick walkway (left). Stone gazebo (above) is used for ceremonial dais. Ceremony in progress (below).

161

focus is solely on your event. Prior step by step planning with the support staff is available seven days a week and assures perfection the day of your celebration. The staff is eager to assist clients in personalizing their event. Rest assured every whim is catered to by the Maitre D' and Bridal attendant.

Through the most state-of-the-art digital tech-

show and special effects. Opt to enhance the magical memory of your first dance as you and your newly-wed seemingly float amongst a heavenly-lit low-lying cloud. As the party progresses, selected moments of your special day are broadcast "Live" on a retractable nine foot projection screen.

The Estate can provide entertainment. Both their

Indoor ceremony (opposite). Newlyweds (above) seemingly float amongst a heavenly-lit low-lying cloud–part of The Estate's elaborate high-tech effects to enhance special celebrations.

nology, The Estate produces a theatrical scene set to rival any Broadway production. Captivate your guests as Bride, Groom, and Bridal Party are introduced through a symphony of musical notes perfectly sequenced to accompany a dazzling display of luminescent beams. Through one remote switch, shades effectively darken the Grand Ballroom, enhancing the effects of their lighting

fabulous house band and DJ (who often work together) have been performing at The Estate for six years and enjoy a wonderful reputation.

The Estate at Florentine Gardens is nestled on four acres and is located at 97 Rivervale Road in River Vale. For additional information or to tour The Estate, call (201) 666-0444 or visit the website www.florentinegardens.com.

The Clubhouse. Photographs courtesy of Bill Stores Photography. Soaring ceiling and dramatic light fixtures within the clubhouse (opposite).

The Architects Golf Club

Architects is the region's one-of-a-kind, semi-private facility. Its newest addition is a 16,000 square foot clubhouse distinctly designed for fine dining and corporate and social occasions.

The clubhouse boasts a spectacular 4,000 square foot grand ballroom and restaurant featuring panoramic views of 175 acres of lush fairways and rolling hills. Whether you are golfing, hosting a corporate event, or celebrating a milestone, a pledge of first-class service follows your every step.

The day you say "I do" is perhaps one of the most important. Architects treats it as such - attending to every detail to ensure you enjoy the day as much as your guests. Expect only the finest of service at every turn. The cuisine will be exceptional and the setting breathtaking. Your affair will be the only wedding celebration planned for the day, making Architects feel like your very own personal country club.

Architects' clubhouse amenities include a bridal suite, a stunning bluestone patio for ceremonies and cocktail receptions, as well as flexible menu packages. This will offer you the opportunity to tailor the event to your specific needs.

The clubhouse also includes Thyme Restaurant and Bar, a French-inspired casual however, upscale dining experience in a impressive venue highlighted by a soaring ceiling, cozy fireplace, and stunning outdoor terrace.

Architects is New Jersey's only legacy golf course. It is unique in that it embodies 70 years of design styles and offers a history lesson in golf course architecture, honoring greats at each hole. Owners Lawrence and Dennis Turco of Turco Golf Inc., along with parent company Grasskeepers Landscaping, partnered with Golf Course Architect Stephen Kay and *Golf Digest* Architecture Editor Ron Whitten to unveil this distinctive course.

Like a private country club, Architects caters to its customers by offering a state-of-the-art practice facility and instructional programs provided by a qualified PGA professional. Architects has been recognized by numerous notable publications for excellence in hospitality and golf operations. Architects is located at 700 Strykers Road in Lopatcong. For additional information call (908) 213-3080 or visit the website www.thearchitectsgolfclub.com.

Thyme Restaurant and Bar (left) and Bridal Suite (right).

Bride and Groom make a fairytale appearance in a Cinderella Carriage.

Bear Brook Golf Club

Bear Brook Golf Club is nestled in the beautiful rolling hills of Sussex County and winds through the eighty-six-home community of Bear Brook, just fifteen minutes from I-80. The 11,000 square foot clubhouse, which opened in Autumn 2006, offers everything you could want or need to make your visit memorable. Whether it's a casual round of golf with a few friends, an anniversary party of 100 guests, or a business meeting with 30 colleagues, Bear Brook is a perfect venue.

Golfers enjoy an 18-hole championship golf course and practice greens, full service pro shop, and men's and ladies' locker rooms with shower facilities. While open to the public, Bear Brook Golf Club offers a limited number of membership opportunities along with an array of tournament packages. You can relax with a drink after your round on the wrap-around veranda overlooking the 18th green or grab a bite in the Bear's Den grill room.

The gracefully designed clubhouse provides a unique setting for your next party, business gathering, or wedding celebration. The dining and meeting rooms, as well as the Bear Brook Lounge, offer spectacular views of tree-lined fairways and wooded terrain. Brides will appreciate the outside wed-

Clubhouse, fairway view, and banquet table setting.

ding ceremony site and spacious bridal dressing room. Bear Brook is also the perfect atmosphere for a rehearsal dinner, bridal shower, bachelor party, or wedding brunch. Their full-time event coordinator will attend to every detail of your meeting or special occasion, adding a personal touch with extraordinary menus, décor, music, and service. Handicap access and wireless Internet connection round out the host of amenities.

It is said, "Each visit to Bear Brook Golf Club provides an experience that is certain to bring you back again and again." Bear Brook Golf Club is located at1 Players Boulevard in Newton. For additional information call (973) 383-2327 or visit the website www.bearbrookgolf.com.

Borgata
Hotel Casino & Spa

Whether there for business or pleasure, Borgata's guests are treated to the ultimate in hotel accommodations, dining, gaming, and entertainment. With 125,000-square-foot casino, specialty retail shops, destination restaurants, a 54,000-square-foot spa, salon, event center, The Music Box theater, and exciting nightlife options, Borgata offers the unique experience of being in the center of it all. Your choices for celebrating are almost limitless at the Borgata.

It's far from business as usual when companies hold their meetings and conventions at Borgata in Atlantic City. With its 70,000-square-feet of event space, state-of-the-art technology, and on-site event planners, Borgata offers a business destination that can

Entrance to Bobby Flay Steak.

Ballroom pre-function room.

feel and function like a vacation retreat.

Borgata's meeting and convention facilities range in size to accommodate almost any group. The Event Center features 30,000-square-feet of column-free space with a capacity for 2,400 guests theater-style, 2,000 guests for seated banquets, and 3,700 guests for a stand-up cocktail reception. Meetings begin in the adjacent 5,800-square-foot pre-function space. Dramatic 30-foot ceilings and a 2,000-square-foot stage can disappear automatically, to provide all the theatrics and space versatility necessary for ensuring a memorable event. The Event Center also offers an advanced sound and projection system, broadcast-ready media-rich technology, and a reception bar area.

Borgata's 20 meeting rooms accommodate anywhere from 10 to 3,700 guests. Available rooms include one 12,000-square-foot venue that accommodates 1,900 guests for receptions, or 1,300 seated; three 4,500-square-foot rooms that accommodate 600 guests for receptions or 290 seated; four 1,250-square-foot rooms accommodate 180 guests for receptions, or 99 seated.

The 10 boardrooms at Borgata can be arranged in a variety of configurations and feature ocean views, marble foyers, large plasma screen TVs, and cabinetry with wet bar. Eight studio boardrooms are 800 square feet each, hosting 12 to 41 guests. Two 550 -square-foot rooms provide space for 16 guests each.

Beyond Borgata's traditional meeting facilities, there are several unique venues for groups. Outdoor events can be staged around Borgata's scenic verandas and reflecting pools with seating for up to 300 guests. An indoor courtyard also provides panoramic views of the gardens and many of the restaurants have unique private space options.

Celebrated chef Michael Mina brings his superlative seafood and signature classics to Borgata with SEABLUE. This Bon Appetit "Chef of the Year 2005" made his East Coast debut at Borgata. Known for his thoughtful and innovative flavor combinations and signature "trio" presentations, Mina strives to present cuisine that combines unique flavors and presentations with classical techniques. A twist on a familiar favorite is his two-pound Maine lobster pot pie with truffled lobster cream and seasonal vegetables. Besides a large dining room and lounge, featuring a blue-veined marble bar, two additional spaces accommodate 20 and 45 guests for private parties.

Special events at Old Homestead Steak House are tailored to the guest's needs and preferences. For a minimum charge of $1,000 for 10 persons, private parties can order from the regular menu or have Chef DiBona create a special tasting menu for the table. This very personal dining experience begins with a consultation with the chef, followed

Acclaimed chef Michael Mina of SEABLUE.

Elegant entrance of Luke Palladino's Specchio. Sister restaura

by some of his recommendations according to the preferred tastes of the group. Those who opt to let Chef DiBona choose their meal for them have been happily presented with inventive and luxurious selections such as Foie Gras with strawberries and balsamic reduction, American Kobe Strip Loin carved tableside, Kobe Beef Ravioli, and Whole Lobsters poached in beurre monte. Large diver scallops, caviar, truffles, and hamachi are also popular ingredients for DiBona's tast-

Abstract bubble motif exterior of SEABLUE.

the passages below.

Private room at Old Homestead Steak House.

ing menus. Celebrities such as John Bon Jovi, Alice Cooper, Ethan Hawke, and Sopranos cast member Vincent Pastore have all experienced the chefs table at Old Homestead Steak House at Borgata.

Omaggio, one of two private rooms tucked inside Luke Palladino's popular restaurant Ombra, accommodates 10 to 120 guests offering a selection of more than 14,000 bottles of wine, along with extensive wine and food tasting menus.

Wolfgang Puck American Grille offers two multifunctional, private dining rooms (50 seats), which can open onto Puck's first-ever Chef's Table in the kitchen, an excellent space for parties and private gatherings.

Borgata's banquet and catering facilities provide the same level of culinary excellence found in Borgata's restaurants. Executive Chef Ron Ross oversees the dedicated catering kitchens, as well as all breakfast, brunch, lunch and dinner services plus catered refreshment breaks. Ross custom-designs all menus for any buffet and banquet event, while Borgata's remarkable restaurants also offer special menus to accommodate groups. Borgata Hotel Casino & Spa is located at One Borgota Way in Atlantic City. For additional information call 1-(866) MY BORGATA or visit the website www. theborgata.com.

A brass plate denotes arrival to Bretton Woods.

Bretton Woods

The house, built in 1894 by Oscar Coles Ferris and his wife Louise, was designed after the Ford Mansion in Morristown. Historic records indicate that this is no coincidence as Louise Ferris was the granddaughter of Jacob Ford. Oscar Coles Ferris and Jacob Ford were both well known financers of the 19th century. Their joint efforts helped to create the First Bank of Morris County, as well as many other business activities vital at the turn of the century.

Today, Ferris House has been renamed in honor of the United Nations Monetary and Financial Conference of 1944 (known as the Bretton Woods Conference) at which

An elegant deck affords pristine view of nature and provides peaceful location for cocktails.

time gold became the world's monetary standard.

The gracious and intimate lobby offers a hint of the elegance to come at Bretton Woods. While your guests are welcomed by the warmth and charm of a stately colonial mansion, the bride and her party share precious moments together in her own private bridal room. Your wedding ceremony is a world away at Bretton Woods. Exquisitely manicured gardens offer privacy and beauty that embrace your special day. The grounds changing with each season will enchant you.

Your guests will delight in nature's perfect point of view. Cocktails are served on the elegant deck overlooking a beautiful expansive lawn and charming carriage house. While inside, your guests will partake of a sumptuous hors d'oeuvres buffet.

Let all wedding dreams come true in the splendor of the magnificent Grand Ballroom. White glove service and spectacular cuisine create a dazzling celebration full of memories to have and to hold. Evening falls and the magic of Bretton Woods illuminates from the enchantment of old world gas lamps and the spectacle of trees adorned with thousands of twinkling lights. Bretton Woods is all a glow with romance.

Winter is a wonderland at Bretton Woods. You and your guests will be swept away to a bygone era replete with the warmth of crackling fireplaces and the charm of Colonial America. This idyllic setting, reminiscent of Courier & Ives, is perfect for your holiday celebrations.

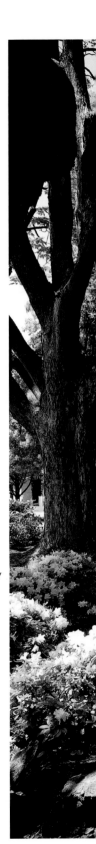

Grounds set for ceremony (left) and, pictured at right, is Bretton Woods in spring.

Bretton Woods—a place for all seasons.

Bigger isn't always better. At Bretton woods, they understand that not every business wants to host their important affair at a large conference hall. For those smaller, more intimate events Bretton Woods offers your company a cozy setting in a stately colonial mansion, gracious service from an expert staff, and a personalized, home-like atmosphere in a location convenient to your place of business.

For events such as board outings, stockholders' meetings, new-product launches, retirement dinners, holiday parties, barbecue picnics, outdoor cocktail receptions or even just to honor your employees for a job well done, Bretton Woods is unsurpassed in bringing style and flair to corporate events. Whether your party consists of 10 people or 100, you're guaranteed to find exactly what you need to show your employees how important they are to you. A complete audio/visual department maintains flip charts, overhead projectors screens, VCR, DVD, monitors, microphones, and Internet access.

Bretton Woods is located at 361 Speedwell Avenue in Morris Plains. Call (973) 538-9000 or visit the website www.brettonwoods.net for more information.

Cozy fireplace room set for an intimate cocktail party.

Piazza di Roma

*P*iazza di Roma is a superior banquet facility enhanced by gourmet cuisine, beautiful landscaping, experienced in-house entertainment, and welcoming personable service. A long tenured staff brings every detail together, producing distinguished celebrations full of lasting memories.

The elegant and seasonally decorated banquet rooms can accommodate intimate parties of 30 to banquets for 300–all custom tailored to suit your individual needs and budget. Piazza di Roma is ideal for weddings and banquets for all occasions, including anniversaries, corporate functions, quinceaneras, engagement parties, rehearsal dinners, holiday parties, communions, on-site ceremonies, christenings, bar/bat mitzvahs, and birthdays.

As you pass Route 34, your attention is drawn to a picture perfect lawn and vibrant colors emanating from plush flower beds surrounding Greco Roman statues. It is the passion of the in-house landscaper that creates this multicolored sensation. Guests are able to savor the beauty of scenic gardens nestled behind the establishment. These gardens are fitting for a romantic ceremony, photo shoot, or a scenic open air cocktail party. The grounds are meticulously maintained and

Above, setup for cocktails outdoors in the garden, and a stylish table setting in main ballroom. Below is a collage showing the manicured grounds and a wedding ceremony.

are an ideal backdrop for any special occasion.

When it comes to weddings, it's one at a time. Total commitment allows the staff to pay precise attention to details and work as a team focusing on the success of your event. The whole facility, staff, kitchen, management, and owner are all dedicated to achieving this goal.

Total Sound is the in-house full service entertainment company made up of professional entertainers adept at emceeing a party. Their entertainers set the mood for a festive good time. State-of-the-art

sound, lighting, and video simulcasting elevate any celebration.

Specializing in Italian cuisine but offering much more, Piazza di Roma puts a premium on high quality food. Choose from a variety of garnished hors d'oeuvres passed butler style on silver trays such as herb encrusted lamb chops, mushroom caps stuffed with crabmeat, and skewered tenderloin marinated in a ginger teriyaki sauce. Some of the specialties for dinner receptions include sole stuffed with crabmeat and scallops topped with a herb butter lemon sauce and filet mignon draped in a brandied mushroom sauce.

Owner and operator Rosalia Randazzo will person-ally oversee every detail of your affair. She is a highly experienced caterer continuing a family tradition in the food service industry. Piazza di Roma has a reputation for the finest cuisine, excellent service, and personalized attention—all ensuring your affair is a unique and memo-rable occasion for all. Piazza di Roma takes the worries out of party planning by providing everything from limousines to favors. Each year during the week of Valentine's Day, past brides and grooms are invited back for a special celebra-tion that has become an enviable tradition.

Piazza di Roma is located at 1178 Highway 34, in Aberdeen. Their phone number is (732) 583-3565. Visit the web site at www.piazzadiroma.com to see their beautiful gardens, full menu offerings, testimonials from past clients, and more.

Valley Brook Golf Club

Valley Brook Golf Club, nestled amongst scenic fairways, gorgeous greens, and picturesque ponds, offers the perfect setting for catered events year round. This lavish setting accommodates social and corporate affairs up to 120 guests, and golf-outings as large as 150 or intimate parties as small as 50. There are great choices of fine cuisines, often customized to your taste by their resident executive chef. A fully-stocked classic bar and fine wines complement each occasion, and an attentive staff provides superlative service to the last detail.

They have only one affair at a time. The breathtaking panoramic views are an ideal backdrop for many celebrations and events, including weddings, holiday parties, rehearsal dinners, class reunions, anniversaries, christenings, communions, baby/bridal showers, and more.

The Guarino family, specializing in fine dining and quality cuisine for over thirty years, is highly regarded in the food service and catering industry.

Paul Guarino, Sr., a graduate of the Culinary Institute of America and winner of the prestigious Crystal Pineapple Award for Catering Excellence, continues to excel with his progressive and innovative approach in serving the ever-changing tastes of his clientele.

The Guarino legacy is continuing into the twenty-first century on a challenging course to exceed its history. Currently, Paul's children, Paul Guarino Jr. and Nicole Guarino are involved in the day-to-day operation of the business. The Guarino family takes pride helping people celebrate life's most important milestones and promises your wedding will create memories that last a lifetime when celebrated at Valley Brook Golf Club. Their professional staff and personalized service will assure an event that is sheer perfection.

Valley Brook Golf Club is located at 15 Rivervale Road in River Vale, N.J. For additional information call (201) 666-2080 or visit the Guarino's multi-location website www.colonialinnnj.com.

The Ballroom (opposite). The clubhouse's patio (opposite bottom)–a popular site for cocktail receptions. (Below) Scenic view from the outside veranda.

Chapter 6
Culinary Pleasures

Lounge in Il Villaggio's new banquet facilities. Guests are just beginning to arrive for a wedding reception.

Flower filled urn mural in background of ballroom table.

Il Villaggio

This iconic ever popular Northern Italian restaurant has recently expanded; elaborate banquet facilities were constructed, adding large catered affairs to Il Villaggio's distinguished list of services. This monumental transformation marks a new chapter in the success story of this bastion for fine dining. Elegant, contemporary, lavish, and sizable all fittingly describe the new addition.

Enter through thick glass plate doors and behold, a two-story foyer. Peer further ahead; the lounge will grab your attention. Murals depicting trees and Gothic sculptures at dusk rise high on both sides of and amazing bar constructed from beautiful swirl accented green granite imported from India. The new lounge is ultra-chic and sophisticated. It prompts a desire for champagne or up-glass martini.

Proceed leftward, a corridor hung with Victorian style chandeliers, will guide you to two banquet rooms. The main ballroom is magnificent. Tasseled velvet drapery extends floor to ceiling. Murals of English gardens are center stage in this room accented with gold tones. Five dramatic crystal chandeliers hang from high above and plush custom carpeting encircles a marble dance floor.

Also to the left, if you're in the bridal party you may ascend the staircase to the bridal suite. It is spacious and beautifully accented with fine furnishings, matching chandeliers and wall sconces, and private marble powder room. A wrought iron railed Juliet balcony overlooks the main banquet room. It is ideal for tossing the bouquet or peering in on arriving guests.

It's refined elegance throughout the facility. Crystal chandeliers imported from Italy, solid mahogany doors and woodwork throughout, and marble floors make an impressive statement. Your guests will be moved by the surroundings, gracious service, and exceptional cuisine.

Even before the new addition, Il Villaggio was a prime site for both social and corporate special occasions. Each year they host thousands of businessmen and women, who recommend Il Villaggio to their colleagues as the perfect restaurant for an intimate business meeting. They were acknowledged in *New Jersey Monthly* Magazine and voted "Best Business Dining." Il Villaggio is an ideal venue for corporate business

Main ballroom as seen from Juliet balcony.

Bartender Kelly O'Connor and the impressive green granite bar. (Opposite) The party begins.

dinners, corporate business luncheons, and client entertaining.

Il Villaggio opened its doors on December 1, 1979. Since then owner Ralph Magliocchetti, originally from Rome, has consistently provided guests with truly memorable dining experiences. Il Villaggio has a stellar reputation for exceptional cuisine. Seafood arrives daily from the Fulton Fish Market. Veal dishes are extraordinary and meat is dry-aged. The wine list received *Wine Spectator* Magazine's "Award of Excellence," and specializes in Italian and California wines.

Accent piece on furnishing displaying guests seating cards.

Today Ralph Magliocchetti operates Il Villaggio with his three daughters, Angela, Maria, Anna, son-in-law John Yessis, and a very seasoned staff, many with twenty to twenty-five years tenure. In response to such admirable dedication and consistency, a second generation of customers has made Il Villaggio home.

Il Villaggio features classic Northern Italian dishes, as well as a wide variety of fresh seafood specials that change daily. Some of their most celebrated dishes include a double-cut veal chop ala Aldo, chicken scapariello, linguine malafemmina, and an enticing seafood salad. Il Villaggio's dessert menu features homemade selections of ricotta cheesecake, tiramisu, zabaglione, and crème brulee. Aside from the regular menu, their experienced chef will gladly accommodate requests for dishes of your own creation. If you prefer fine dining in the comfort of your own home, take-out is also available.

Il Villaggio is located at 651 Route 17 North in Carlstadt. Lunch is served Monday through Friday; dinner is Monday through Saturday. Il Villaggio is available for all social and corporate parties, up to 250 guests, seven days a week. For additional information call (201) 935-7733 or visit the website www.ilvillaggio.com.

III Amici

amily owned and operated, III Amici Ristorante has a distinguished reputation for fine catered affairs and Northern and Southern Italian dining. Weddings, business luncheons, holiday parties, and more are accommodated in one of several newly remodeled banquet rooms designed to host 25-200 guests. The recent renovation has given a whole new luster to III Amici. Everything from an all new entrance, imported Italian chandeliers, fine drapery, black and white granite flooring in the banquet room, and new chairs contributes to a refreshing style of luxury and elegance. The lounge, featuring live entertainment on weekends, is accented with an attractive tin ceiling and wall length mural of Venice. Outdoors, a new cascading fountain and beautiful landscaping welcome your visit.

Chef Owner Giovanni Lavorato began his culinary studies at the age of fourteen and received a culinary degree in Italy. He then traveled and cooked throughout Italy, France, Switzerland, and Germany. In 1967, Lavorato immigrated to Montreal, Canada, and began working in one of

the most famous Italian restaurants in Canada, the Bianca Franco.

When Lavorato came to the United States in 1968, he continued to work in the restaurant business, and in 1975, established the Appian Way Restaurant in Orange. There he received acclaim and recognition in *The New York Times*, *The Star Ledger*, and *Gourmet Magazine*. After eight years there, Lavorato bought the Bel Vedere in Clifton and also received recognition and awards. In 1990 he opened III Amici Ristorante, and in 1995, was awarded the Man of the Year award by *Il Ponte Italo-Americano International Cultural Magazine*. This award commended Mr. Lavorato's achievements and leadership in the food service industry.

Today, it is a family operation at III Amici. Giovanni is joined by son, Dante as the general manager, daughter Teresa as the office manager, and Giovanni's brother, Mario, as head chef. For catered affairs the Lavorato

(Above) One of many conversation pieces and fountain view (left).

Main banquet room (above). Tableside service trolley and close up ornate garnish work (below).

family and friendly wait staff cater to every desire, including flowers, choice of linen colors, customized menus, a fantastic array of desserts, and delightful fine Italian and Continental cuisine.

III Amici Ristorante is located at 1700 W. Elizabeth Avenue in Linden. Lunch is served Monday through Friday. Private parties and dinner are available seven days a week. The phone number is (908) 862-0020. Additional information can be found on the website www.amiciristorante.com.

189

Clockwise, from above – Wines are a part of the Angelo's experience. An afternoon party in progress. And a large table setup, apropos for a rehearsal dinner and easy communication amongst guests.

Angelo's Fairmount Tavern

*I*n addition to being one of Atlantic City's most cherished restaurants, affairs of all types are catered at Angelo's, including weddings, holiday parties, corporate events, bar/bat mitzvahs, christenings, birthday celebrations, and convention parties. Along with numerous expansions over the years, many new private banquet rooms have been added, each one presenting its own unique atmosphere. For off-premise catering Angelo's provides delicious food, excellent service, and even entertainment. Angelo's also can provide multi-media equipment and computers to create a most effective business meeting or presentation.

Angelo's Fairmount Tavern is an ideal location for wedding receptions. Their weddings and banquets manager is dedicated to bring you the wedding reception event of your dreams. From small intimate family gatherings to large gala events, Angelo's can accommodate 25-225 people in their three banquet rooms. The banquet staff will assist you in planning your special event, from a light buffet to a complete sit-down dinner.

Angelo's Fairmount Tavern was founded in 1935 in the Ducktown section of Atlantic City by Angelo Mancuso. Today, Angelo's is a landmark, one of the most successful restaurants in Atlantic City. While other restaurants have been hurt by the influx of casinos, Angelo's has flourished. Their success is a testa-

ment to the Mancuso family's dedication to serving their customers. The restaurant is now run by third generation family members who continue the winning formula

The most popular dish at Angelo's, lobster ravioli with a seven-ounce warm water lobster tail done with fresh spinach, fresh diced tomatoes, and jumbo lump crab meat in a homemade lobster cream sauce.

Coffee service.

Luncheon setup.

Wedding reception table setting and head bridal table.

started by Angelo Mancuso.

Details are looked after here. The coffee is from Naples, and aged steaks are seared on the edges first to ensure juices are locked in. The sauce is made from Grandfather's secret recipe. Employees also have the same caring attitude, many with over ten year's tenure. Angelo's was voted "locals" favorite, "Best Italian," and "Best Dining Institution" in Atlantic City Magazine. A large menu features many long-time favorites, as well as many new and creative specials.

The menu at Angelo's offers a bounty of choices. They offer dependable, inexpensive dining in an atmosphere full of history and friendly service. The cuisine is Italian. Specialties include seafood.

Enjoy appetizers of eggplant Florentine topped with sautéed spinach, provolone cheese and marinara sauce; portabello mush-

192

rooms with jumbo lump crab meat in a scampi style sauce; fresh mussels in their famous marinara sauce, fra diavalo, or in white wine sauce; antipasto; and scungili salad made with succulent chunks of conk served cold with spicy vinaigrette dressing.

For entrees enjoy lasagna, manicotti, classic raviolis, and eggplant parmesan. There are many chicken favorites, including marsala, pizzeola, and cacciatore. Veal dishes include veal lightly floured and sautéed in lemon, butter, white wine, and a touch of garlic; parmesan style–breaded and topped with provolone cheese and smothered in red sauce; and a large 14-ounce veal chop char-broiled to perfection and topped with tri colored peppers in a burgundy demi sauce. Their savory 16-ounce aged steaks, all cooked Sicilian style in a seasoned cast iron pan, include Maryland style, topped with jumbo lump crab meat, bleu cheese, and gorgonzola cheese and ala Angelo, with roasted peppers, sliced black olives, and artichoke hearts in balsamic vinegar.

Enjoy their selection of wines by the glass or full bottle. Homemade desserts include Italian rum cake, carrot cake, apple walnut pie, banana cheesecake, homemade ricotta cheesecake, white chocolate raspberry tartufo, and more.

Angelo's Fairmount Tavern is located at 2300 Fairmount Avenue (first right off Atlantic City Expressway and just two blocks from the Atlantic City Convention Center) in Atlantic City. Lunch is served Monday through Friday and dinner and private parties are available seven days a week. The phone number is (609) 344-2439. Additional information can be found on the website www.angelosfairmounttavern.com.

"The Villa" room (above). Once an alley way between two buildings (below), now part of bar area with vaulted roof.

Biagio's

iagio's Ristorante and Banquets, a family owned and operated establishment for 20 years, provides a beautiful atmosphere and attentive friendly service for both exceptional catered affairs and leisurely dining. Recently completing a major addition, Biagio's added a new banquet room. It's really a transformation that gives an exciting new look to the whole facility which now has three private rooms for catered events. The new edition has given Biagio's the ability to do elaborate weddings and larger functions for their corporate clientele.

The new banquet room features fine mahogany woodwork and a custom crafted built-in mahogany bar. Plush carpeting surrounds a granite and marble dance floor. The entrance is completely private and valet parking attendants await your arrival. The room accommodates weddings, birthdays, showers, meetings, christenings, retirements, bar mitzvahs and bat mitzvahs, office parties, anniversaries, and comfortably seats up to 160 guests.

Biagio's originally opened in 1987. At the start, Biagio's was small; however, great food built an

ever increasing clientele and several expansions followed. Teddy and Jimmy were meticulous about using only the freshest ingredients to make their homemade sauces. Their vodka sauce, marinara sauce, and salad dressing thrilled patrons. Today, Teddy's and Jimmy's sons and a daughter in-law have joined the family business. Rest assured, whether having a catered affair or a meal in the restaurant, the Perides family will be looking after you and providing a memorable experience. Guests at Biagio's get treated like family whether they are having a dinner or a fancy affair.

Teddy's son Jimmy is the chef. He has contributed a lot of depth to the selections offered by introducing modern and innovative specials to the restaurant's classic Italian and American menu. He is a Johnson and Whales culinary school graduate and has been mentored by both Master Chef Nino D'Urso and Chef "Molto

Mario" Batali. He also received training in Italy and worked at Café des Artistes in New York City. Jimmy's wife, Paula, is the banquet manager and custom designs parties for customers.

The wine list is hand picked by sons Jimmy and Teddy and features California and Italian wines and also includes select wines from regions all over the world. New wines by the glass are featured monthly. Yearly, there are four sought after wine dinners featuring elaborate wine paired courses. Both sons Jimmy and Teddy studied wine at the famed wineries in California.

The restaurant features two fireplaces, a wine room, and large usually bustling lounge.

Biagio's is located at 299 Paramus Road in Paramus. Biagio's is open for lunch, dinner, and catered events seven days a week. For additional information call (201) 652-0201 or visit www.biagios.com.

Architectural drawing of new front exterior (above left).

Ribbon cutting ceremony with the town's mayor and the Perides family in attendance (above right).

Celebration in the background of wedding cake (above left) and arched opening view of dining room (above right).

Don Quijote

*D*on Quijote is known for generous portions, gracious service, and a masterful touch with Spanish cuisine. Several expansions and a propensity to continually enhance their décor have kept this restaurant moving forward over their seventeen-year history. A recent renovation has added a large banquet room, embellished with a crystal chandelier and decorated with colorful Spanish artwork. Large arched windows create an airy atmosphere. Beautiful stone tiles,

One example of the Spanish artwork beautifying Don Quijote (above left). A wait staff member at a lobster and seafood station (above).

handcrafted woodwork, and new entrance doors have further enriched the surroundings. Their banquet room has seating for up to 150 people and future plans for 300. Private parties catered run the gambit from fanciful weddings and business functions, to showers, rehearsal dinners, and holiday parties.

Stop in any time of day on a Saturday and Don Quijote will be whirling with activity. From the time the doors open, customers keep flowing into this restaurant.

The food at Don Quijote is the foundation of their success. Their Spanish cuisine has garnered much praise from critics and built a legion of regular customers. *The Record* rated Don Quijote "Excellent," and said, "Good food made with good ingredients is what counts in Spain and also at Don Quijote. Virtually every dish we sampled was fresh, well-made, and nicely presented." The menu comprises a vast array of seafood entrees, shrimp dishes, fish, meats, and poultry selections. Favorites include garlic shrimp, mussels in green sauce, paella, mariscada, lobsters, 1¼-3 lbs. (weekends 10-20 lb. available), shrimp with wine sauce, whole red snapper, filet mignon Don Quijote served with a brandy mushroom sauce, and chicken villaroy with a Bechamel sauce. Nightly specials have included stuffed veal chops and risotto with shrimp, clams, scallops, and mushrooms. Don Quijote creates an unhurried relaxed cordial atmosphere where their magnificent cuisine can be enjoyed to the fullest.

Don Quijote is located at 344 Bergen Boulevard in Fairview. They are open seven days a week for dinner and private affairs and serve lunch through Saturdays. Private parking and handicap accessibility adds to the convenience. Off-premise catering brings authentic Spanish cuisine to your location. They also transact a large take-out business. Their web address is www.donquijoterestaurant.net. Phone number is (201) 943-3133.

Don Quijote's waiters (right) deliver the popular flaming steak and provide wine service.

The main ballroom known as The Madison Room (above). Pictured below and right are the culinary team in action, the garden at night, elaborate cakes, an ice sculpture, and fanciful table settings and decorations.

The Empire Club

Nestled on a quiet residential street, this newly redecorated facility boasts all of the charm and elegance found only in the finest European hotels and clubs. Exclusively yours, The Empire Club offers one wedding at a time, featuring a large separate room for cocktail hour and the ceremony. The Madison Room is the main ballroom and comfortably seats 230 for a dinner reception. The award-winning cuisine is presented and served in the most impeccable manner and the experienced team is capable of customizing any menu. Your guests will be pampered by a most experienced service staff and your whole affair orchestrated by a well-versed maitre d'.

John Giuffre is a graduate of the Culinary Institute of America and the owner and operator since 1995. He is the former owner of the ☆☆☆½ Trebbiano Restaurant in Nutley. John is committed to only the highest standards of service and cuisine. He will personally make sure that your affair is nothing short of perfect.

Other amenities and services provided by The Empire Club include an outdoor garden, bridal suite, valet parking, and in-house party planning. The Empire Club is located at 136 Mehrhof Road in Little Ferry. For additional information call (201) 641-2892 or visit the website www.theempireclub.com.

Wedding cake by Frungillo.

Frungillo Caterers

*T*he Frungillo Family continues its innovation in all aspects of catering, from cuisine to service and hospitality. Now in its fourth generation, the family business, operated by Robert and Gerald Frungillo, maintains a commitment to client satisfaction by

Three members of the Frungillo service staff with a plated rack of lamb. Pictured at left–The palatial Castle at Skylands Manor.

offering unique and spectacular locations along with exciting menu choices and professional polished staff at all of its locations or at events at the location of your choice.

The Castle at Skylands Manor has become one of New Jersey's premier bridal destinations. Explore 100 acres of formal botanical gardens within 1,000 acres of natural woodlands that make up The Castle at Skylands Manor. Stroll across rolling lawns, verandas, and stone terraces that provide the perfect ambiance for a ceremony, cocktail reception, or party.

The historical National Newark Building.

Enjoy the magnificent view of Shepherd Lake from the private chapel. Taste Frungillo Caterers' incomparable culinary delights and warm hospitality as you are swept away by the elegance of this manor house. Skylands offers a magnificent bridal suite that every bride can enjoy for the day.

Built as a Tudor showplace in the popular style of Eclecticism, the vast interiors display late Gothic to early Renaissance architectural styles. Formal gardens can accommodate up to 600 guests, the Grand Ballroom up to 230, and the entire castle up to 300.

The Villa at Mountain Lakes is designed in a classical architectural style, with light, open spaces which invite a sense of warmth and charm. The Villa is truly a place for celebrations and special occasions where each detail has been thoughtfully designed to accommodate exclusive and distinctive events. The interior features a private dining room and formal living room with classic furnishings and a fireplace. Events at The Villa have the luxury of private cocktail rooms that open to a beautiful pond and waterfall gar-

The Mezzanine.

den. Hand painted ceilings adorn the ballroom, while tastefully displayed artwork and antiques add to the ambiance and celebratory feeling of this unique mansion. Hospitality and exceptional service are the cornerstone of the philosophy behind the success of The Villa. Romance abounds! From the moment your guests arrive they will be greeted by fine valet captains and then welcomed by a friendly smile from your personal hostess.

(Opposite) The Great Hall and the formal gardens at The Castle at Skylands Manor prepared for a ceremony.

Candles and fresh flowers are abundant. Maitre d' and white gloved staff are at your service to enhance the beauty and comfort of your special event at The Villa at Mountain Lakes.

The Mezzanine, located three blocks from the New Jersey Performing Arts Center, is one of New Jersey's newest and most spectacular ballrooms. The award winning building has undergone a transformation which has restored it to its classic Art Deco style. Receptions at The Mezzanine are hosted one event at a time. The grand setting with imported marble and thirty foot vaulted ceilings gives The Mezzanine a real "chic" Manhattan style social feel. Whether your affair is for 150 or 900 guests, the staff and ambiance at The Mezzanine will exceed your expectations.

The Oakeside Mansion is a nineteenth-century estate with unique charm and beautiful English gardens. Nestled among three acres of beautifully landscaped grounds, The Oakeside is a twenty-three room mansion available exclusively for your special occasion. Guests enjoy a quaint feeling as they view the grounds from the glass enclosed garden room. Warm paneled walls, fireplaces, and an indoor fountain add to the charm that is abundant at the Oakeside Mansion. Choose the permanent garden tent for up to 210 guests, the mansion for up to 120 guests, or the entire estate for 350 guests.

For more information on any of the Frungillo properties or catering services, please visit the company web site at www.frungillo.com or call (973) 256-9380.

(Opposite page, clockwise from top) The Villa at Mountain Lakes, The Villa's Grand Ballroom, the entry foyer at The Villa.

(This page, top to bottom) The Oakeside Mansion, wedding doves at Oakeside, hosts Robert and Gerald Frungillo with Linda Pergola and Joe'l Guarino.

Newly remodeled, La Catena's glowing exterior at dusk.

La Catena

*L*a Catena provides an intimate atmosphere for private parties, corporate events and meetings, and fine dining. A recent renovation created a flashy exterior that becomes a dramatic shimmering beacon in the night sky. Private spaces were also added giving more opportunities for those who have grown accustomed to celebrating important occasions at this refined establishment.

Family owned and operated, you could say it all began in Italy when the owner's grandparents had there own restaurant of the same name. La Catena means chain and signifies a small bridge in Italy, known as the "Bridge of the Chain." The family used the bridge regularly to cross over a canal. La Catena stateside has been in business for seventeen years and innovatively prepares Northern Italian cuisine, which *The Star-Ledger* gave a ☆☆☆½ review.

All the amenities, from comfortable dining chairs, beautiful chandeliers, and fireplaces to intricate woodwork, fine linen tablecloths, fresh flowers, and soft music playing in the background creates an old-world charm throughout the dining room and private party rooms.

Enjoy enticing fare. There are creative dishes like prosciutto wrapped monkfish and classics like the house specialty veal chop stuffed with fontina cheese, prosciutto di parma, and sautéed in a sherry wine mushroom sauce. Desserts can intrigue as well, like their fried ravioli dessert stuffed with sweetened ricotta, chocolate sauce, and ice cream. Great wine is part of the experience and La Catena's wine collection offers a host of fine wines including Super Tuscans, Chianti Classicos, Barolos, Barbarescos, Amarones, Brunello Di Montalcinos, and many more.

Elegant private rooms can accom-

modate 12 to100 guests. The larger banquet room's soothing ambiance arises from crystal chandeliers, an old-world intricately crafted fireplace, and artwork depicting vessels sailing across calm waters. Another smaller private room has a hand painted mural and wine display. La Catena is located at 966 East Route 22 in Bridgewater. For additional information call (908) 725-9300 or visit the website www.lacatena.com

The new banquet room (above) accommodates both social and corporate affairs and can comfortably seat up to 45 guests.

Hand painted murals and a display of fine wines (left) distinguish this boardroom style space used for a variety of intimate gatherings.

The Landmark

The Landmark is located in the heart of the Meadowlands in East Rutherford, New Jersey. It is in close proximity to most major highways, making it convenient for guests traveling from northern and southern New Jersey, as well as New York City. The Landmark takes pride in providing your guests with exquisite cuisine and impeccable service. Their exclusive Tuxedo and White Glove French Service, combined with ethnically diverse menus, will appeal to the eyes as well as the palate. Wedding menus can be customized to various ethnic tastes; The Landmark specializes in Italian, Spanish, and Caribbean cuisine. For the past 30 years The Landmark has catered thousands of Bar and Bat Mitzvahs and has become famous for "kids free."

Separate cocktail lounges with sunken bars are available for private cocktail hours; adjacent dining rooms are elegantly decorated with crystal chandeliers, soft tone wall coverings and ample dance floors accommodate up to 300 guests.

The Landmark's multi-lingual staff will see to your every need and cater to your guests' every request. Your affair at the Landmark will make a lasting impression and create memories to be long cherished while helping you celebrate one of life's joyful landmarks!

The Landmark is located at 26 Route 17 South in East Rutherford. The staff can be contacted at (201) 438-3939 or Catering@Landmarknj.com and the website is www.landmarknj.com.

The Warwick Room.

The Continental Room.

The Garden.

209

Oven roasted pousson with baby vegetables (above). Photography provided by Verdini Studios.

Luca's

Luca's Ristorante, with locations in Somerset and Flemington, has succeeded in creating the seemingly unattainable: a modern interpretation of time honored family recipes that translates effortlessly into a contemporary dining experience. The culinary distinctiveness of brothers Luca, Andrèa and Daniele DiMeglio is apparent in all aspects of their business approach–from unique homemade offerings to an inventive translation of traditional Italian fare and ending with imaginative dessert creations.

Born and raised in Ischia, a small island off the coast

210

of Naples, Andrèa and Luca grew up around an Italian dinner table and quickly developed a love for home cooked meals and the fresh ingredients of the island. After moving from Italy to New Jersey and opening Luca's, the brothers decided that the only way to give their customers a real taste of what they loved was to bring it all here for them to experience first-hand. Since then, Luca's has been the site of a visual and culinary destination of authentic old-world Italian cuisine, specializing in extraordinary dishes that come straight from the heart.

While both locations show modest exteriors, it's what is inside that is worth the trip. The ambiance of the restaurant is the result of the DiMeglios traveling often to their home of Ischia and bringing back pieces of authentic Italian décor–all with the goal of recreating the comforts of their Italian home. Immediately upon entering the restaurants, the result of their efforts is apparent: you are transported to a warm and rustic Italian café, complete with hand-painted terracotta wall tiles, Tuscan style wooden table and chairs, hand wrought candelabras and wall sconces, and numerous displays of characteristic pottery.

Prominent Italian home furnishings merchant, Tuscan Hills in Princeton, is the resource for much of Luca's décor items, glassware, and accessories.

While fine food is the obvious hallmark of a great restaurant, Andrea and Luca recognize the need to offer their guests an exceptional dining experience that encompasses all aspects of a visit. Outstanding service is a key component of the culinary journey at Luca's, and servers are highly trained professionals who recognize the importance of treating each guest with the utmost of attention and consideration. And no detail is too small when you're treating guests as family in your home…. from fine stemware and flatware to handcrafted glazed earthenware dishes… the difference is obvious and it's clear that every aspect of the experience matters.

Both chefs also acknowledge the difference that the origin of their food, as well as the preparation and presentation of each dish, can have on the overall dining experience. Selecting the highest quality of imported foods such as buffalo mozzarella and tomatoes from the rich soil near Mount Vesuvius, ensures that their dishes carry the mark

Prosciuotto wrapped scallop on baby vegetable tower.

Flemington location.

of authenticity. Pasta dishes, baked and served in bright earthenware, are made using regional cheeses and the highest quality pasta from Naples. Gnocchi, ravioli, and stuffed shells are handmade by Luca and Andrea on the premises, and Luca's relies on the local quality of Jersey Fresh farm grown vegetables from C & M Produce Company.

Private parties, special events, and innovative gourmet tastings round out the offerings of Luca's Ristorante. For guests seeking a secluded retreat to celebrate any special occasion, Luca's can

Bufala Caprese

Somerset location.

Handcrafted three-dimensional Ponchinello object d'art from Ischia.

accommodate private parties up to 70 guests. Customized menus and personal service with meticulous attention to detail are trademarks of an event at Luca's. For clients desiring a more lively event to mingle with other guests, Luca's also hosts exclusive wine tastings and chef demonstrations. For any dining experience requiring the utmost in service, quality, and value, Luca's Ristorante has an innovative and inspired solution. For more information, contact Luca's Ristorante in Somerset at (732) 297-7676 and Luca's Ristorante in Flemington at (908) 284-9777. The addresses are 2019 Route 27 South in Somerset and 319 Walter Foran Boulevard in Flemington. The web address is www.lucasristorante.com.

Grilled veal chop with butternut squash.

Créme brulée.

The Yasmeena Darbar (above), an executive dining room for 24 guests. (Below) Dining room at Lawrenceville location, (609) 689-1500. (Opposite) Grand entrance of Lawrenceville location. —Photos courtesy of Verdini Studios

Palace of Asia

Over a period of 25 years Palace of Asia has developed expertise in catering for wedding receptions, corporate affairs, and all types of events ranging from small first year birthday parties to huge conventions comprising over 8,000 guests from all over the country. Their skillfulness in coordinating and catering large weddings is highly recognized and has received accolades from hosts as well as their guests. Several generations have now enjoyed Palace of Asia's fine services that relies on over 100 years of family recipes. In addition to their own outstanding facilities, they work with prestigious banquet facilities in New York, New Jersey, Pennsylvania, Delaware, and Connecticut, accommodating 100

The fine silk and elaborate decor used for an event in the banquet room at the Cherry Hill Palace of Asia, (856) 773-1200.

able of all ethnic foods because of terrain, climate, and the infusion of people of many different religions into Indian culture over thousands of years.

The taste that people savor in an Indian dish may range from the delicate to the hearty, the piquant to the fiery. Americans think of most Indian cookery as being of the latter category. However, it is the inclusion of one ingredient, chilies, which makes food "hot". By toning down the use of chilies, as well as the richer ingredients, Palace of Asia offers recipes that are gentler, but retain the flavor, aroma, and texture for which Indian cuisine is rightfully famous.

Palace of Asia presents a wide selection of Indian haute cuisine made from the finest and freshest ingredients. Their menu offers a welcome change from the ordinary that is not only pleasing to the palate, but a healthful alternative as well, owing largely to the use of a variety of vegetables and leaner meats. Frequent visits to Palace of Asia and savoring different items on the menu will make you a connoisseur of exotic Indian cuisine.

When you think of India… it conjures images of royalty and legendary hospitality. Inspired by the architecture and ambiance of the royal courts of India, the ownership presents a restaurant extraordinaire. The Palace of Asia, located in both Lawrenceville and Cherry Hill, offers ornate dining rooms embellished with intricate designs. Immerse yourself in the ambiance of rich Indian culture and traditions while relishing the finest cuisine developed by owner and nationally renowned master chef, Sukhdev Kabow. Palace of Asia Cherry Hill has dining and banquet facilities. Palace of Asia Lawrenceville is a 240-seat, full-service restaurant and includes an oversized lounge with dining tables, a main dining room, and an executive dining room (Yasmeena Darbar) for 24 guests that is ideal for large groups and business meetings. Indulge yourself at the Palace of Asia and they promise you Nirvana!

For off-premises catering that is authentic with grill and clay oven, contact the Director of Catering & Marketing at (609) 631-0800/ Cell (609) 865-3231 or visit the website www.palace-of-asia.com. Palace of Asia is located at 540 Lawrence Square Boulevard South in Lawrenceville, (609) 689-1500 and 2389 Marlton Pike (Rt. 70W) in Cherry Hill (856) 773-1200.

to 3,000 guests. They are always gracious and happy to assist you in finding a suitable facility for your function.

Indian cuisine is among the most varied and enjoy-

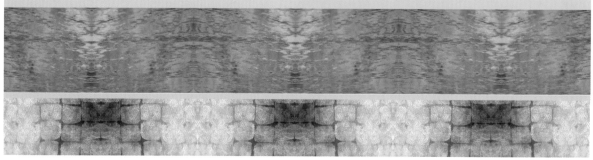

Index

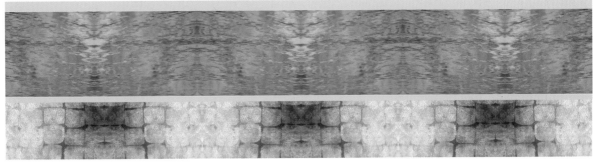

Index

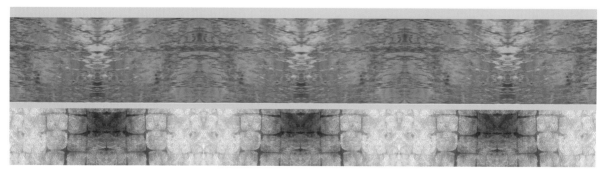

Index

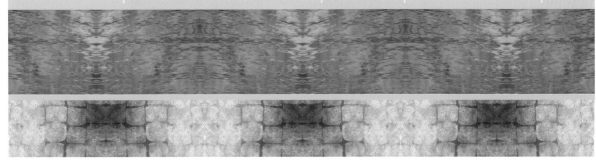

For additional information on the
featured facilities in this book and
a continuing exploration of
New Jersey's Top Places
for Catered Affairs,
visit www.TopPartyPlaces.com

Also by NJR Publications

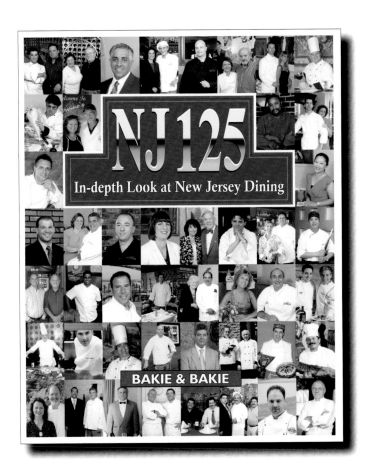

Tour New Jersey's finest restaurants. Over 600 full-color photographs, 256 pages, and ten chapters explore everything from Grand Restaurants, Exotic Cuisines and Steakhouses to the state's most Distinguished Chefs and Wine Savvy Restaurants. NJ 125 is an in-depth look at remarkable dining across the Garden State.

Pick up at local merchants throughout the state or visit www.njrpublications.com for a location near you.

Cover Price $19.95